STUDY
in
LILAC

—

MARIA-
ANTÒNIA
OLIVER

—

TRANSLATED BY

KATHLEEN
MCNERNEY

—

THE
SEAL
PRESS

—

Published by arrangement with Edicions de la Magrana, Barcelona.
Originally published in Catalan as Estudi en lila.

Publication of the book was made possible in part by support from the
National Endowment for the Arts and the Department of Culture of
the Generalitat of Catalonia.

Library of Congress Cataloging-in-Publication Data
Oliver, Maria-Antònia.
    Study in lilac.
    (Women in translation)
    Translation of: Estudi en lila.
    I. Title. II. Series.
PC3942.25.L53E813   1987   849'.9354   87-20516
ISBN 0-931188-53-9
ISBN 0-931188-52-0 (pbk.)

Cover illustration by Jana Rekosh.
Cover design by Deborah Brown.
Printed in the United States of America.
10 9 8 7 6 5 4 3 2

PREFACE

Maria-Antònia Oliver (Manacor, Majorca, 1946–) belongs to an unusual cooperative: writers of detective stories who collectively sign their books with the name Ofèlia Dracs. "Ofèlia" takes her inspiration from a number of Americans who wrote in that genre: Dashiell Hammett, Erle Stanley Gardner, and Raymond Chandler, to name a few. "Her" work has been a tremendous success.

With this apprenticeship, Oliver published her first detective novel, *Study in Lilac* (*Estudi en Lila*), in 1985. Bringing her feminist point of view to the genre, she addresses the problems of crimes against women and shows their struggles to go beyond victimization. The role of detective Lònia Guiu as mediator and problem-solver is most compelling; her reactions of frustration and triumph, hostility and sympathy, give this novel its human dimension.

The action takes place in and around Barcelona, a city well known to artists, tourists and sailors, and more recently to planners of Olympic Games. Its role in the Spanish Civil War is also well known, thanks to George Orwell and many others. But its importance as the capital of Catalonia has often gone unperceived by foreign visitors and been denied by non-Catalan Spaniards.

The language of this small country is Catalan, a Romance language like French or Italian, whose linguistic history follows a similar pattern, with its first texts dating from the 12th century. Its first writer to achieve world recognition was Ramon Llull, a 13th century mystic. At present the language is spoken by 6 million people in Catalonia, Valencia and the Balearic Islands, a number that puts it ahead of the Scandinavian languages and nearly on a par with Greek. As in all languages, there are dialectical variations in the different Catalan-speaking areas.

In literature, Catalan has an active and strong tradition in spite of periodic severe repressions. Barcelona is the capital in the world of publishing, both in Catalan and Castilian. In addition to the great number of titles published every year written originally in Catalan, there are also many translations into Catalan from English, French, German, and other languages.

Barcelona today is a bilingual city. As a major industrial base of the country, it has a high percentage of immigration from poorer areas, particularly Andalusia. More than ten years after the new autonomy laws, it still struggles with "normalization" of the language. Not unlike in Quebec, the difficulties of bilingualism are intensified in Catalonia by hostilities between the two sides and memories of oppression.

Maria-Antònia Oliver has written a number of other novels and short stories; she has just completed a sequel to *Study in Lilac* in which Lònia, on a well deserved vacation in Australia, finds new clues to an old mystery. Lònia will also be the protagonist of a series of detective stories on the radio, after which the readers will be invited to call in and help solve the crimes described in the programs.

I would like to thank the Department of Culture of the Generalitat of Catalonia for aid in financing this project and Carles-Jordi Guardiola for help in bringing that about. Special thanks to the generous Junoy family; Carme of Lloret de Mar and Carme of Sant Julià de Vilatorta, for putting me up in those two lovely places while I was working on it. For help with the work itself, many thanks to Patsy Boyer and John Martin for reading and smoothing out the rough spots in English, and to Montse Reguant for explaining some obscure expressions in Catalan. Most of all, thanks to Maria-Antònia Oliver, who patiently explained, sometimes more than once, passages I found difficult; she's the best Catalan teacher I've ever had (or was it Majorcan?).

Kathleen McNerney

PART ONE

I

Monday Morning
"Did she have any friends in Barcelona?"
Tearfully the woman handed me a crumpled piece of paper. The handwriting was decisive, not at all refined. Don't worry, it said. Don't feel bad on her account. And don't look for her.

The envelope was postmarked in Barcelona, so the mother had taken the first boat, it's the first time she's left Majorca and to have to do it because of this, my god! No, not that she knew, she didn't have any friends in Barcelona, but who knows, Holy Virgin, now she sees how little she knew about her daughter, because she never would have suspected that she would run away from home like that, and what if those people had gotten hold of her who turn girls into . . . , and the sobs shook her whole body.

"Don't worry, I don't think so," said Jerònia with an expression that for the mother was assurance but for me a question.

Uncomfortable, I shrugged my shoulders; I didn't like these inescapable commitments, nor these hysterical clients who come in convinced that people like me are fairy godmothers loaded with charms to solve all their problems.

The mother described the clothes that were missing from her daughter's closet, gave me a few photographs, and left, calmed down by the fact that since I was a woman, and a Majorcan like her, I would surely try harder to find her. And above all, be sure to tell her that if she doesn't want to come back, she doesn't have to, but at least don't leave the family in chaos like this.

"Her father and I can't sleep, or talk about anything but her, and the neighbors are already asking us about her and we don't know what to say as an excuse, what a scandal, my god! if the word gets out."

The two women left, closing the door softly and my partner, who had been trying not to laugh during the visit, burst into guffaws.

"I don't think it's funny. We'll see how this girl ends up, if we ever find her."

"No, I'm not laughing at that. It's just that when you talk with Majorcans, it sounds like you just got off the boat. Here you speak perfect Barcelonese, no accent, but when you get together . . . "

"If your ears were finer-tuned, you wouldn't find my Barcelonese so perfect. And I'm proud of it."

"Okay, okay. . . . Who is that Jerònia?" and he started laughing again. "Some weird names you guys have: Apol.lònia, Jerònia, and this kid Sebastiana . . . . Who is Jerònia?"

"You're an ignoramus. You sound ridiculous trying to imitate my accent. You're a circus clown, Quimet."

He was a good guy, though. I'd run across him at the gym, when I was taking a course in self-defense. He was the teacher's assistant, and they couldn't stand each other for some reason I still haven't been able to figure out. Quim's informalities went overboard; he showed up when he felt like it and did the job just as he pleased. On the other hand, the instructor paid him whenever he felt like it. His job ended when I finished the training; so, following a charitable impulse, I offered him a job with me. With the condition that he not put up any conditions. He only put one: I shouldn't ask about his personal life—above all, I shouldn't demand any answers.

"Now don't get mad . . . "

"Jerònia is a former colleague from the agency in Palma. . . . One day I ran into her and I told her I had started my own business in Barcelona. . . . At the time she was taking courses in Social Work."

It had been a long time since she and I had worked together at the Marí Agency, Commercial and Confidential Reports. We worked in the office, editing the forms that informers filled out. Mr. Marí visited banks to offer the services of his new business, his son did the most sensitive stuff, a few retired Civil Guards

4

filled out forms with the information that buyers of refrigerators and TVs on time gave them, which we edited into the proper form. And when, tired of the monotony of those reports, we would start chatting, Mrs. Marí would come around, Lady Maria, who was doing chores in the kitchen, and bawl us out for not slaving away enough; vigilant as she was of the interests of the family affairs, she even made sure that we didn't go over the half hour we were allowed for a snack, even by half a minute, and if it was under, all the better.

And now that same Jerònia who used to wipe off the telephone receiver with a handkerchief soaked in cologne because it stank—Mr. Miguel Marí lisped a little and spat abundantly—had brought me a client from the neighborhood where she was a social worker. A small-town woman who had moved to the city and was looking for her missing fifteen-year-old daughter. A case like so many. We'd found scads of them, girls like her. From small towns and big cities, especially lots from outside of Catalonia. Some of them had gone off with girlfriends and they felt free without doing anything sensational, happy to believe they were on their own. Others were terribly homesick and went home, sometimes accepting humiliating conditions from their parents. Still others had fallen into the cash trap and when their parents found out that they were dishonored, they repudiated them completely. And of course there were the ones we never did find.

I had decided not to take any more cases like that, because my office was starting to look more like a refuge for stray kids than a detective agency, and I was getting tired of being a babysitter. But this was sort of a duty.

"Of course, your friend Jerònia, and your little heart that beats when you hear the accent from the island . . . "

Before I had time to tell him to go to hell, we heard some discreet knocking at the door, as if whoever it was hadn't read the sign Come In.

"Come in."

The door opened and I was assaulted with the disagreeable fact that the office, in spite of a recent paint job, was old and shabby, and that the Miró poster which dominated the scene would never look like an original, in spite of the framing job.

Usually, clients go directly to Quim's desk, whether they're male or female. But she headed straight for mine, and when she approached me, I worried that I hadn't put on enough deodorant that morning.

She was one of those women whose presence reminded you that you should go get a haircut one of these days, and as the lady from the Ladies Auxiliary to the Falange used to say, moderation is the key to elegance.*

I'm sure she didn't turn the heads of men on the streets, but, my god, what class! In the end the moderation seemed exaggerated, as if she wanted to hide the brilliance of her glamour, which only expert eyes would be able to appreciate, under a mask of discretion. Not a jot of makeup; I almost wanted to offer her my lipstick collection. Smooth hair, completely natural, but cut so perfectly that it betrayed an excellent hairdresser and lots of daily care.

"May I help you?"

"I'm looking for three men," and she handed me a piece of paper with a figure on it.

"Sit down, please."

It was infernally hot. Even my watch was too much, and I had to wipe the sweat from my chin and neck from time to time. Quim's forehead was steaming. But it seemed that the temperature had no effect on her, as if she were above those human miseries.

"Who are they?" I looked at the figure, trying not to make my curiosity too obvious.

"That's why I came to you, so that you would find out who they are. All I have is this license plate number. From Barcelona. A metallic green car. I don't have any idea of the model or year."

"Why do you want these three guys?" Quim interrupted, full of self-confidence. But the woman looked at him so haughtily that my partner was crestfallen.

"It's highly confidential," the woman said to me.

* The Falange was the Spanish Fascist Party, in power from 1939 to 1975 under General Franco. Its Ladies Auxiliary undertook the task of imposing an acceptable traditional code of behavior on the young women of the nation.

"There are no secrets between Ms. Guiu and myself," Quim said, recovering from the blow. "You may speak in confidence."

Before she had a chance to request to speak to me alone, I took the initiative.

"Quim, please."

Quim got up, dawdling over a few useless papers at his desk and some on mine, which he put carefully in a folder, and he went to the bathroom, which was the only other room in the office.

"So why do you want to find the three men?" I asked.

"Must I tell you the motives? You find them, I'll pay what you ask. . . . "

Had Quim gone to the bathroom so he wouldn't hear that?

"I need to know where I fit in, madam. I don't want to lose my license for nothing."

"It's not a sordid affair, I can assure you." She took out expensive cigarettes and a gold lighter. Her fingernails weren't painted, but they were manicured.

"No, I don't smoke, thanks."

It occurred to me that I really should get an ashtray for clients who smoked, and I discreetly removed the No Smoking sign.

"I'm an antique dealer, and these three men bought a very valuable piece from me." Strangely, the cigarette smoke didn't bother me. "They paid me with a check from an account that had already been closed. It's a considerable amount."

"Didn't you get confirmation from the bank?"

"I took down their identification card numbers, their names and addresses. I thought that would be enough. Besides, it wasn't banking hours."

"And then?"

"Everything was false. But my employee had sense enough to take down their license number."

"Whose name was the account in?"

"He had died years ago."

"Do you have the check? It's another lead, besides the car registration. How the checkbook came into the hands of those individuals. . . . "

"I tore it up. It wasn't useful to me anymore."

She made a childish gesture of excuse, which didn't go at all with the poise of such a self-confident woman.

"What bank was the check drawn on?"

"I don't remember . . . oh, yes, it was not from Catalonia, because to deposit it I had to endorse it as out of state."

"But checks from branch banks also need that endorsement. So you remember that it was not from Catalonia, but you don't remember what bank it was. Do you remember, at least, your own bank, madam?"

"Is this an interrogation?"

Not finding an ashtray, she put out her cigarette on the floor. She placed her hands on my desk and she looked me straight in the eye.

"Do you want to take my case or not, Ms. Guiu?"

"Why didn't you go to the police? The police . . . "

"If the police could solve all the cases," she cut me off, "what would detective agencies be good for?"

She brushed the back of her hand over her mouth, a gesture I often made to wipe sweat from my upper lip without being obvious. Her chin was shining.

"I want discretion," she went on in a different tone of voice. "I'm sure I can solve this problem satisfactorily, either getting my money or the piece returned. If I put the affair in the hands of the law, I might have the satisfaction of seeing all three behind bars, but that satisfaction doesn't interest me, I can assure you, if it means wasting my time, and losing my money and the statue."

A wooden statue, modernist, unique. The antique dealer's voice kept its agreeable and convincing tone, but I kept thinking that the piece she was describing so carefully and lovingly was on some shelf in her home, that the check with a dead bank account owner from a forgotten bank had never existed, and that the three men were really only one. That the car owner was a one-time lover who had abandoned her and who she, for whatever reasons, wasn't prepared to lose. It wasn't a new story; I had found myself involved in similar ones. A story as tawdry as the one of the stray Majorcan girl, or more so.

"Okay, we'll look for the three men."

After all it was a job, and it was clear that I didn't have to do it for the motives that she set forth to me. And there wasn't any danger at all of getting involved in things that would be dangerous to my career.

"Give me your name, address and telephone where I can get hold of you easily, and I'll get to work... "

"I just want you to find them," she cut me off again. "Find out their real names... and take photos for me so I'll know it's them... and where I can find them.... "

"At the moment the car registration is our only lead." I had already discounted the check. "And if the car wasn't stolen, we would only find one of them. Unless they live together."

"That's why I want the photos. Get pictures of the owner of the car and the men he hangs around with. And don't talk to them until I've identified them.... "

I'm used to playing hardball, and giving orders. Her authoritarian tone of voice bothered me. But I decided to go for it.

As she spoke she took a card out of her purse. I've always liked snakeskin purses, but they don't go with my usual outfit or my bank account.

She left the card on my desk and got up.

"And if at the moment we only find one of them, then we can talk about how to find the others. Or maybe it won't matter," I suggested.

"Of course," she said distractedly. "Good-bye, I'll be waiting to hear from you."

She didn't give me a chance to say that those subterfuges weren't necessary. Nor that I usually didn't accept my clients telling me how to do my job. But the truth is that I liked the gal so I hadn't said anything like that even though she was there for quite a while. It was fine that she hadn't told me her sordid story as if I were on the other side of a confessional or a social worker. I could leave that up to Jerònia, whose vocation was helping others, and I would do my own job.

I heard the toilet flushing—more noisily than usual, as if Quim had really yanked it.

Just as Mrs. Elena Gaudí closed the office door with the same gentleness with which she had opened it, he came out, annoyed and sweaty. The odor from the bathroom cut through the cloud of the perfume the new client had left behind.

"What did that amazon want?" With one hand he wiped his sweaty brow and with the other zipped up his pants.

"Don't tell me you didn't hear every word. And she's not an amazon. You men wear blinders, pal. If women don't spell everything out, men never seem to catch on. And would you do me the damn favor of zipping up your pants inside the bathroom? Even in that way you men show off your sense of power."

"Hey, hold that steam-roller tongue of yours. If you're mad at the lady, get mad at her, okay?"

"I'm not mad at anyone. It's just that sometimes male indiscretion gets to me."

"Now you're talking like Mercè. But I'm glad you recognize me as a male. I've been plenty discreet already today. Don't you think it's asking a lot to be on the throne all that time?"

I imagined him sitting on the toilet, trying to listen to the conversation, and I burst out into genuine laughter.

"And now you're laughing, crazy lady."

"Did you hear her, or not?"

"Of course!"

"She really made up a story! But it reeks of a love story and nothing else."

"Ha! She's too skinny to have love stories like that! That she didn't tell you the truth is clear as a bell, but don't make up romances, Paloni."

"Don't call me Paloni, dammit!"

"Paloni is much more exotic than Lònia, dear! And don't tell me to call you Apol.lònia. You sound like a Roman empress if you don't shorten your name."

"I just don't like the sound of it, and that's all. It's a romance, I'm telling you. But did you get a good look at that lady?"

"No way. I like the flashy ones, myself."

"You don't have your eyes in the back of your head, pal. You've got them on the end of your . . . "

"Discretion, sweetie, discretion!"

And we started to map out the job. Quim bawled me out for not having insisted on more information about the check, and for not having asked for a description of the three men.

"If I already know it's a story . . . why press the point?"

"That's the very reason, see?"

He was surprised when I put him in charge of the lost girl and I took on the job of the antique dealer.

"Just find out if the card she left me is genuine, and not another trick, and that's all you have to do. I'll do all the rest."

"I can't understand it! What would Jerònia think if she knew you left the case she recommended in the hands of a servant?"

In the end, Quim was as curious as I was about Mrs.—or Miss? Gaudí. He was clearly playing it cool; he wasn't as blind as he wanted me to think. But it was me who had the license, the office, and who paid the yearly fees; I called him a partner because I wanted to, but in reality he was hired help. So I was the one who chose which job to do, and distributed the others. I was more interested in the antique dealer than in the girl. I wanted to know why she had lied to me.

II

Tuesday morning

The metallic green car finally came through the main gate. Those quiet streets on the city's hillsides made me nervous. All with imposing high walls enclosing gardens, that captivating odor of plants well watered the evening before, not a single car around to make mine less obvious, not a soul on the street, except an occasional maid in uniform, and worst of all, not a single store with window displays to gaze at.

The gardener, or doorman, or whoever it was, closed the door and the car skimmed smoothly down the street. Too late it occured to me that he could have been useful to me.

"Heavens, what a vehicle!" Neus got three shots of it, from the front, the side, and the back. "It's worth thirty grand at least."

It was a tasteful car, though. In spite of the metallic green and Neus' economic assessment. And a woman was driving it, though it was registered in a man's name.

Silence and boredom returned. Neus covered the lens. "Not yet," I said indifferently. "Let's wait a little longer."

"How much do you charge for not doing anything?"

"I manage OK. How about you? Can you make it on your photos?"

"Well, it depends. Sometimes you get a well-paid reporting job. If you get still photos from a film, it's great for a couple of weeks. But it's not as easy as what you're doing."

"You'll have to teach me a little. A detective who can't take pictures is only half a detective."

And a detective who can't tell a Citroën 2CV from a Porsche,

12

too. And a detective who is afraid of weapons, too. What kind of a detective was I, anyway? Because a detective who gets depressed when she has to spend a few hours waiting isn't a detective, she's a jerk.

Deep in those dark thoughts, I almost didn't notice that the main gate was opening again.

The characteristic crunching of wheels on gravel announced a slowly approaching car, and the time that passed before the black, majestic black car emerged meant that there was a good distance from the garage to the gate.

Neus took more photos from the front and the side, but the glass of the back window was tinted.

"All closed up, in this heat!" I exclaimed.

"Cars like that are air-conditioned, dear. Go on, if you pull up a little I can get one of the other side, and maybe that way we can discover something clear in the laboratory."

"Get the doorman first."

There almost wasn't time.

"A shitty shot!" she grumbled, her professional pride wounded. "I hope it won't be blurry! You could have told me before that you wanted the porter too."

While I followed the big black car waiting for the opportune moment to pass him, Neus kept on grumbling.

"It seems to me that you aren't too sure what you're looking for, right?"

"A man, but I don't know which one."

"Shit, me too, isn't that too much? But they don't pay me for doing it!"

I laughed without commenting. I liked Neus. She was crazy, uncomplicated and happy. I wondered where she could have gotten that folk-rock style of hers, that explosive and fun mix of girl scout and punk aggression.

"Wait, it's better to follow the car until it stops. When the owner gets out you can get a better picture. . . . "

I enjoyed weaving through the avalanche of traffic. Following a car through the ocean of vehicles in Barcelona was a challenge for me, and I hadn't lost one yet. I didn't know a thing about types and models, but I was an expert behind the wheel.

Neus was clutching her camera and staring at me in fright.

Her lips were pursed. From time to time she would just say "Christ!" her voice trembling as she hunched over in her seat on my side.

We were going full speed down Balmes Avenue. Before reaching the Diagonal the big car put on its right turn signal. Seconds later, Neus had attached the telephoto lens and was shooting continuously. The chauffeur had gotten out and was making the useless gesture of opening the back door, because the owner was already half out. Photos, photos, photos.

"The chauffeur too, Neus!"

The cars behind us started to get impatient because mine was blocking their way. I got out all upset and raised the hood, poking around the mysterious workings of the motor, while Neus took all the photos she wanted of the car owner, the men who greeted him, the chauffeur who got back into the big car, and everyone who entered or left the building.

The horn-honking was so intense that it overwhelmed the heat. It was beginning to get dangerous because it attracted so much attention to us. Neus was well hidden inside the car, but it was already too risky to stay there. So I acted like I knew what I was doing with engines, closed the hood, and walked around the car.

If the ranter behind us who was shouting silly obscenities with his congested face hanging out of the window had known that my car trouble was faked, he would have had a stroke. I solemnly gave him the finger, got into the car and started up.

Tuesday evening

"Did you find her?"

"Do you think you Majorcans give off a special scent so hounds can find you?"

"Don't be gross, Quim."

"Jerònia called seven times. I told her you were on the track so she would leave me alone. The antique dealer called too, and I told her the same thing."

"Would you investigate this company?"

"Is it her sweetie's?"

"I assume so."

14

"But, she only wants the photos and the addresses. If it's just a romantic tiff, I don't know why you're getting so obsessed with it."

"I like to do the job right."

"You're in charge, boss. Right away."

He took the name of the business I had written down and left me the list of items covered in the search for Sebastiana. It blew me away how much he had done in one morning. Quim was a jewel when he wanted to be. Too bad his inspiration to work lasted for such short spurts. And too bad all that work hadn't done us any good yet.

I called Mercè.

"It's time for your checkup, Lònia," was her greeting.

Besides being my gynecologist, Mercè was a priceless collaborator with me in cases of lost girls. And without charging. Well, let's say we helped each other. She and a few other women in her field dedicated themselves to dealing with cases of unreported rapes, desperate abortions, and things like that. Her information had helped me find more than one girl in trouble, the daughter of intransigent parents or the victim of unscrupulous lovers. And vice versa.

"Listen, I have a case of a Majorcan girl. . . . Yes, that's right. . . . No, nothing yet. . . . "

They also had a more or less clandestine network—not at all official in any case—against irresponsible professional behavior. "There are too many women in the world without ovaries," she had told me. "And it isn't always necessary to take it all out, just easier! Afterwards the hormonal dysfunctions start and who knows what psychic complications." Her radicalism made my head swim, and that's why I put off my checkups as long as I could. She hassled me: You have to come more often. The way to avoid problems is to solve them before they become serious, just a cytology in time . . . and she never charged me anything, but she did deliver some feminist sermons that made me aware of problems that I hadn't ever thought about. I would leave her office so depressed, I felt silly for not having seen all the evidence I had right in front of my eyes. . . .

"I'm sending you a photo and a description of her right away by messenger. If you find out anything, let me know at once. . . .

Yes, but at the moment I have another case on my hands and I don't know how long it'll take. Okay, that's fine."

She put the nurse on and I made an appointment.

I wondered for a few seconds whether to call Mrs. Gaudí, but I decided to wait until tomorrow. I wanted to present her with things a little better digested. With another photo session, maybe the three men would become real, that is, if they existed somewhere other than in the lying mouth of my client.

Besides, I'd had enough of women giving me orders for one day—my supply of obedience having been depleted by Mercè and my biannual checkup.

Wednesday morning

Dressed up fit to kill, I made a triumphant entry into the office. Quim's eyes opened up as big as saucers.

"Where are you going disguised like that? I bet you had steak or a filet mignon of crocodile meat for breakfast."

"That's no skin off your ass. What does it have to do with a damn thing?"

"You won't fool anyone with that vocabulary, kid, even if you're dressed up like a Fourth of July horse."

"Do you have the report for me?"

"Yes, but first listen: You look like you lifted those threads from some statue of a saint that broke its neck, and I would even guess Saint Vegetarian."

"Listen, my ideology doesn't have anything to do with my clothes. I'm dressed like this to go ask about making some investments. And I only use that kind of vocabulary with people like you."

"Did you win the lottery?"

"Could there be any better prize than you, darling?"

"Okay, it's up to you. The truth is you look great, Lònia. . . . "

"Do you want to make it with me?"

"Who, me, Lònia? No, thanks." And he tossed the report on the table. "You put too much perfume on."

I grabbed the report. It was written in a doctor's handwriting.

"When will you learn to type, Quim, sweetie?"

"Typing is women's work. . . . "

16

He said it to get my goat. That's why it didn't get to me.

Finesor was an investment company, incorporated with Mr. Felip Antal as major shareholder, president of the board and general manager. That is, he was the whole nine yards. He declared a bunch in properties and deducted plenty of income for charitable works. He was honorary president and had other memorabilia from certain foundations, honorary member of a club in London—we hadn't been able to confirm that information though—married to a baroness of the type who appears in jet set gossip columns... your ideal perfect gentleman.

And Finesor didn't seem to have financial problems.

"So the story about the bounced check doesn't fit in?"

"Right," said Quim.

His voice sounded stuffy because he was holding his nose.

"What's wrong?"

"Your perfume, kid. It makes me dizzy."

"Don't be an imbecile! Okay, if Neus comes with the pictures, have her wait for me. And you can start with the sleaziest pensions. You know the routine."

Mercè had given me leads before on runaway girls, but that didn't mean she would come through this time. We had found runaways before in sordid flop houses, but that didn't mean we'd find the Majorcan either. But those were the first steps, after the hospitals, hostels and massage parlors. If all that didn't work, it would be time to resort to more complicated techniques. Actually, it would be time to psych ourselves up for the failure of the search.

The lobby of the building on Diagonal Avenue was incredibly luxurious. Too much chrome, too much glass, too many uniformed porters, too much carpeting in the elevator. Even the Muzak was too much.

Mr. Antal's company occupied two floors that communicated with each other from the inside. At the entrance, you walked into a new world. No chrome, to begin with. Some pine tables, a sandstone mosaic. It looked more like a place to organize senior citizen excursions or summer camps for kids than an investment company. The atmosphere was trendy and with it. I would have fit in better with blue jeans than with the outfit I was dressed up in. But there was air-conditioning. Too much. My back and armpits were sweaty, and I was getting a chill.

A good-looking, but rather aseptic, young man approached me with a smile intended to be friendly but which was in fact servile. In a corner with rattan armchairs, a man who looked like the type who couldn't even collect unemployment insurance seemed not to have noticed the air-conditioning. He stood up and came over to the young man who had greeted me; his hair was damp, but from impatience, not the heat.

"I'm sorry, Mr. Antal still can't see you," the young man told him in a clipped Spanish which gave away a Catalan accent in spite of his effort.

Despite the simplicity of the decor, the Filipino was out of place in that atmosphere. And he knew it, because he made what seemed an embarrassed gesture; lowering his head, wiping his forehead, he returned to his corner as if he were carrying a load of sugarcane.

Then the guy looked at me, turned his head aside and raised his eyebrows—a gesture half of complicity and half of apology for that human object which had planted itself in the place.

"Come this way, madam," he said, making a bow.

He had me sit down in a wood and canvas chair and sat down himself on the other side of the desk.

"What can I do for you?"

"Well, I've received a good inheritance, and I'd like to invest it in a safe place that will give me income."

"Did one of our clients recommend us to you?"

Luckily, at that moment the Filipino overcame his embarrassment or lost his patience. He had gotten up from his corner and had begun to get insistent, in a loud voice, at the counter that separated the waiting area from the office itself. He wasn't talking to any of the personnel in particular, he was just ranting, with a trembling, strident voice.

Everyone looked at him surprised, and my beardless wonder started moving his hands around as if to tidy up invisible papers on his desk.

From the torrent of words, I was able to get—Mr. Antal, urgent, an important deal, intolerable, wait; the more he went on the angrier he got. The half dozen youngsters scattered around at those desks hadn't been recruited for situations like that one. The people who usually came there must have been well behaved, high class, polite, clean and well dressed—or at least docile. Every time the irate Filipino pounded the counter with his fist, all the lamps on the desks rattled from the blow.

It would have been the perfect occasion for Neus to take pictures; no one would have noticed. And we would have found out more than with just my presence. After all, what the hell did I want at Finesor?

At that moment, a young woman dressed in a fancy silk shift with pearls came quickly down the interior staircase and told the intruder that Mr. Antal would see him. When the man followed her up the stairs, the unanimous sigh of relief from the flaktakers raised the temperature in the room. Calm ensued. Before my dandy had time to repeat his question, to which I didn't have an answer, I went on the attack.

"Do you often have clients like that one?"

"Certainly not, madam. We've never found ourselves in such a disagreeable situation since I've been working here."

"Who is Mr. Antal?"

"The manager."

"The manager receives clients like that one?"

"He's not a customer, as far as I know. He must be a visitor."

"That's even worse, don't you think? Certain visitors, especially if they're not clients, should not be received on the job."

"Well, I really don't know if he's a visitor, maybe it's just an acquaintance."

He was overwhelmed, poor kid. He was looking for a place to disappear. He wouldn't remember to ask me for references.

Why had I come to Finesor? I would have to learn to calculate things better, and not be carried away by intuitions and impulses. After all, what would I get out of talking to Mr. Antal? Maybe a lead to the other two. But was it worth it if the other two didn't exist?

"I don't want to waste more of your time, madam. We mustn't forget the reason for your visit because of that unpleasant incident. You want to invest your inheritance and some savings, right?"

He had recovered his composure, and started reciting the litany.

"That's right."

"Did some friend of yours recommend our company?"

The Filipino came dashing down the stairs. In spite of his anxiety, he seemed calmer than when he had gone up. I came out with another outburst. Maybe that visit wouldn't be as useless as I thought.

"You have a lot of nerve asking for references from decent people who come to ask for your services with people like that hanging around!"

And like a queen, I got up and left the office without reacting to the low-level exclamations of the lackeys.

The Filipino was waiting for the elevator. We went down together. He was very involved with his own thoughts and didn't even look at me. He may not have noticed my presence. So much the better.

He went straight to the bus stop. My car, illegally parked, of course, already had a ticket. So I could leave it where it was, no problem. I lost myself in the crowd.

Waiting for a bus on Diagonal Avenue is torture. The traffic makes the heat worse, stickier. Cars going up and down, so fast. Eyes that don't know how to calm down.

III

Wednesday morning

The city had changed so much since I had arrived here—something only people from outside Barcelona could see. Now, even if you were in a car yourself, the cars bothered you.

One thing hadn't changed: even if they were baking, people still sat on the bus without opening the windows. The odor of perspiration and clothes not washed often enough was also the same. The bus jerking up and down, and its surges to get through the red lights hadn't changed either.

It wasn't until I got off that I thought about why I had gotten on. I was approaching the old quarter following the Filipino—Ponent Street, Leo, then Paloma. I cursed the dress I had worn, not only because of the heat, but also because it made me too obvious.

The badly dyed hair of the stout old whores was pathetic in the midday sunlight. Their shopping baskets made them just like their lower-middle-class neighbors, drudges who hadn't even had time to take their makeup off the night before, overwhelmed, as they were, by housework and putting up with their kids all day long. A few workshops wide open with the hope that a little air would come in gave the sordid atmosphere inside the houses a certain charm.

A group of aggressive girls playing hooky from school took the little work there was that morning away from the professionals, who waited for their customers inside dark bars. The very same owner of the home-cooked food restaurant was opening the metal blinds and hanging the day's menu on the door.

I had lived in this neighborhood when I first came to Barcelona. For three years I lived with a group of Majorcan students in a tiny apartment full of enormous, pretentious furniture. A group of American students lived above us, whom we first suspected of being CIA agents, naturally, but who later became our friends.

In all those years—ten already!—the neighborhood hadn't changed. The walls had a little more of a crust, and the restaurant was much more expensive, because the word had gotten around that it was good and cheap. I had a nostalgia attack that almost made me forget what I was there for. Until then I had followed the Filipino skillfully, automatically, pulled along by a mechanical impulse; now, for a few instants, I forgot I was following him. That's when I asked myself why the hell I was following him.

But then he entered a dark stairway and the door slammed in my face. The doors in the neighborhood had indeed changed; now they were aluminum and glass, funeral parlor style, with automatic security instead of doormen. The doorbell of the second floor had a little handwritten label: Orient Sunshine; a cathouse surely. The druggist looked at me curiously.

"Looking for something, Miss?"

"Doesn't a Filipino live here?"

"Just one? A bunch of them live here, Miss. But they're good people. They say it's an agency for hiring maids. And it seems to be, because at the entrance there's a desk and filing cabinets. They don't cause any scandals, they all look like good girls... Anyway, scandals in this neighborhood, well, we're used to anything nowadays, know what I mean? Besides, they're people too, and they have a right to live, right? As long as they let live, and lately, what with drugs and robberies, we don't live as peacefully as we did before, you work all your life and from one moment to the next you lose everything, maybe even your health, but as you can see, we keep going, and we make it through day by day. That's life, what else can we do? We've seen worse times, and you really can't complain, can you?"

"Do only Filipinos live here?"

"If you mean live, yes, but once in a while some man comes around, you know, white, from here, and some lady... "

"Spanish?"

"And Catalans, Catalans too!"

"What do I do to hire a maid?"

"Ring, call them, and go on up, don't worry, lady. They'll be delighted, the poor slobs! Because they're broke, I can tell you. I know because they buy just what they need, nothing more."

The Filipino was seated behind the desk in the foyer. He looked as though he recognized me, but couldn't remember where from.

"Mr. Antal... sent me.... "

"Mr. Antal?"

"From Finesor."

"Boy, that was quick! He told me it would take a week.... "

His Spanish was garbled with English. And then, there was a silence you could touch, and if you touched it, it jabbed back at you. He was waiting for something from me, and I was waiting for him to keep talking so I could continue the conversation without spoiling it.

From inside the hallway you could hear exotic sounds, bits of words that showed that the Filipinos didn't know Spanish at all, and contrary to what they always told us at school, not much English. A shadow of Tagalog characterized the man's accent, and inside the apartment, Tagalog reigned.

"I like your language... it's full of musicality I'm not used to," I said with a smile.

He didn't hide his puzzlement. He was looking for business and I was coming out with linguistic praises.

"You were at Finesor a little while ago."

I had rekindled his memory. Distrust replaced the confusion on his face.

"Yes, Mr. Antal told me... "

"Are you a partner in the company?"

"No, I'm a customer, and Mr. Antal... "

"Did he give you a message for me?"

"Well, I'd like a maid I could trust, and he said you could get one for me... "

"Mr. Antal sent you here for a maid?"

"Exactly."

I had the feeling the floor was shaking.

"How long have you been a customer of Mr. Antal? Is he your business client?" he said a little ironically.

"What do you mean? Oh, yes... if you can call it a business with us." I was sure my smile looked stupid.

"Yes, of course. But at the moment we don't have any maids available... Maybe in a few days. If you give me your address and phone number, we'll be in touch with you... or with Mr. Antal."

"Okay."

I took a card out of my purse: Victòria Mira, a nonexistent street and telephone number, for just such compromising occasions.

The Filipino accompanied me to the door.

"Do you want me to give some message to Mr. Antal?" I asked as a last resort. The man didn't answer. "Oh, that's right, it's Mr. Antal who needs to give you the message."

He slammed the door in my face.

"So, did you get a maid?" the druggist asked me.

"Not yet, but they'll send me one soon."

"They're good people, like I told you."

From a second floor balcony, a girl watched me leave. I stopped for a moment after I turned the corner at the Plaça del Pedró. I looked up nostalgically; that apartment with the sloped balcony was where the M boys had lived—Miguel, Martí, and Mateu from Lleida. They had married Margalida, Rosa and Catalina, respectively, the last year of school. The year we left our apartment to other students. That was seven years ago. Miguel and Margalida were still together. I had lost track of the other four.

A Filipino girl came around the same corner in a big hurry. Such a hurry she almost ran into me. Maybe it was a coincidence, but it put an end to my reminiscences.

I walked down toward the same street, Sant Antoni, towards Ronda, slowly gazing at the houses like a tourist, turning my head all around. The Filipino girl was obviously following me—too obviously to be true. Halfway down Sant Antoni I crossed towards Cendra Street. I wonder if Lola still lives here? Whatever had become of Elisenda?

Lola was Aragonese and she wanted a good Catalan name for her newborn daughter. And she wanted a spectacular baptism with respectable godparents, she told us. We all named her Elisenda, and many were the nights we took care of her while Lola earned her living as best she could. I decided I would have to return to those streets some other time, without clumsy Filipinos following me, and I started walking faster.

On those streets where the sun didn't shine, the mugginess was dense, dirty. On Riera Alta I went into the same forlorn perfume store where I had bought three ounces of cologne so many times. At that time I wasn't collecting lipsticks yet. It looked as if the place hadn't been dusted since then. The bottles, the hankies, the plastic toys—everything was faded.

I went in and was looking at the lipsticks. It was the same lady, who was just as dusty as the counter. I bought three, of incredible colors, in cases loaded with tacky fake jewels of coke-bottle glass.

The Filipino girl had disappeared from the street. It had been a false alarm. But as I went towards Ronda, a little dark head watched carefully. It disappeared again as I approached.

So I got a taxi when I got to Ronda. From inside, I saw her hiding in a shoe store. She was looking at me with desperate eyes. I felt sorry for her; they would give her hell.

Wednesday evening

"Damn you! It wouldn't have cost you anything to call!" Quim was more a guardian angel than a bodyguard. But when he got like that he was more like a jealous husband or a long-suffering mother.

I weathered the storm patiently. He was right, after all. Neus had been there at noon and had gotten tired of waiting. Quim had gone to Finesor, since I'd had more than enough time to investigate. He had seen my car with a ticket from eleven o'clock. He had gone upstairs, come down, and waited until three. When all the office workers had come out of all the offices, he started to worry about me. So he came back to the office to wait for a call.

"Look, if you had waited a little longer you would have seen me get out of a taxi, get in my car and go home. Besides, you could have taken Neus, who could have taken pictures of everyone leaving the office. And instead of looking for me you could have looked for Sebastiana."

He got furious. I was totally irresponsible; some day he would find me with cement boots on. And when I told him that I had followed a Filipino, he was astonished.

"I don't get it, Lònia, really. Why do you get so involved?"

"Antal is involved."

"So what? That guy's sordid business is not your problem."

What would I get out of investigating him? What was I doing it for? Not Gaudí, right? So who would pay me for the extra work? Gaudí would surely be satisfied with the photos Neus had already taken . . . and besides, hadn't I gone a little crazy, to take photos like that, so openly?

"Who told you that?"

"Neus, of course! She was still bent out of shape from the race you took her on yesterday, to say nothing of the car trouble scene. She told me that if you want any more pictures, you can get them yourself. She doesn't want to get her face busted up."

"She's wishy-washy."

"Anyway, you're playing a TV policeman."

"Policewoman."

"Fuck you."

"Don't you know, dear Quimet, that things done in the open are the least noticed?"

"But when it doesn't work, you're likely to end up with a new face."

"I got out of it, didn't I? And we got the photos, didn't we? How did they turn out?"

"See what you think. Neus wasn't quite satisfied."

"She's a fussbudget."

"A what?"

"Fussy, a perfectionist."

Considering the conditions under which the photos had been taken, they were works of art. Mr. Antal turned out to be very photogenic. Between the smoked glass and the car trouble, I had hardly seen him in person.

I showed Quim the chauffeur and the doorman.

"What a coincidence, huh?" I said ironically. "All Filipinos."

"So, rather than an agency for maids, the agency you dis-covered seems to be for boys."

"Yeah, boy scouts."

"Listen, Lònia . . . "

"Sounds like a sermon coming. Save your breath."

"I'm going to say it anyway. I want to have a clean con-science. Now that you have the photos, take them to the lady. If it turns out that there are really three, and they don't all come out in the photos, she'll tell you to keep on. If she wants more information, she'll tell you. But don't put the cart before the horse. You won't get anything out of it. She won't pay you any more even if you give her a complete biography of the guy. And you have other jobs . . . Sebastiana, a bunch of bank in-quiries . . . "

"Ugh. What a pain."

"But they keep us in business."

"Don't I pay you what I'm supposed to, and on time? Because if you're getting into working conditions, you could have started with that."

"Don't be stubborn, Lònia. You know it isn't that."

I knew very well it wasn't that, even though I paid him next to nothing. But he hadn't wanted a regular job. He said he wanted to come and go as he pleased, without punching the clock. I'm a free spirit, he'd said when I'd proposed that he work with me, and his ingenuous grandiloquence had convinced me. That was almost two years ago, and from time to time he told me he would be away for two weeks. But he always did that when there was just routine work, when I didn't really need him. Why should you pay me, he said, if I'm not working?

He wanted people to think he was hard-boiled, but he was really a marshmallow.

"Hey, I'm taking you out to dinner tonight," I said. He frowned. "To make up for being a pain in the neck today."

"With one condition." Now he was smiling.

"Hey, I'm inviting. I get to make the conditions."

"It has to be a decent restaurant."

"That sure sounds puritanical."

"If you want to eat grass, do it on your own. I'd like a place where I can sink my teeth into a nice piece of meat, rare and tender."

"Crocodile steak . . . ."

I was on the phone until dinner time. Neither hide nor hair of Sebastiana. I left messages everywhere, but it seemed she had never existed. I began to think we would never find her in Barcelona.

Quim had kept on looking in boarding houses. When he came to pick me up, he didn't have any news either. Maybe the girl had already returned to Majorca. Or maybe she was rotting in the bushes along some highway.

"What about Ms. Gaudí?" asked Quim after the waiter had taken his order.

"Tomorrow. We have to make the clients believe our work is hard and time-consuming. Otherwise, they always think it's too expensive."

I watched him as he gobbled up, undaunted, a disgusting bloody piece of steak.

IV

Thursday morning

"Oh, Neus, don't let me down now."

"What if they find out? What if they suspect something and when we get there we find two gangsters ready to skin us alive?"

Her voice sounded shaky on the phone, but I thought I noticed a little excitement too.

"Come on, Neus, give me a break. Do you think we're taking secret pictures of Reagan?"

"I... I already told Quim yesterday... no, no. Besides, I can't let my job go... they'll fire me."

"I'll pay you well, and besides it could be fun. And I promise it won't be dangerous."

The butler looked the part, except he wasn't wearing the striped vest, nor did he have his hair parted in the middle... Too bad.

On one side of the vestibule, dizzyingly spacious, there was a stairway that seemed to be there just for the grand entrance of the star. But since the steps weren't marble and the ceiling wasn't held up by columns, the house seemed just what it was: a house in good taste, not a pretentious cardboard decor.

We had time to look at the paintings and furniture while we were waiting. Signed paintings, old and modern. Authentic. A real Miró, a real Nonell. Old and new combined by expert hands. The decor could be a good conversation piece.

Neus was really having a good time.

"It's like it's from another world," she said, fascinated.

"Fake it. Pretend you do houses like this one all the time."

29

Under a dark, musty painting, without a visible signature, there was a chest. Neus fell in love with it.

"It's as big as my apartment," she said.

"There are a lot like this in Majorca. In the old days, the girls used them for their trousseau. Naturally, we called it The Chest."

"Oh, very clever." She shrugged indifferently.

Under the stairway there was a big chest of drawers with inlay work, hot stuff. On top of it, there was a crocheted dresser scarf that took your breath away. On top of that, a wooden figurine like a Muse from the Palace of Music. The modernist statue.

"Madam isn't quite ready yet. Would you like to come into the sitting room?"

It was a feminine voice speaking an unclear Spanish. Even before I turned around I knew she was a Filipino.

She left us in one of those rooms that you need a maid to keep clean, and take three showers a day to keep from getting it dirty. A soft white modular sofa to sit on. Little white tables; floor, walls, ceiling, and shelves, all white, a collection of books bound in white leather, a white television, white curtains. All immaculate.

"What a precious little room!" exclaimed Neus.

"I'll say."

A few antique pieces placed here and there with great care: an ivory candlestick, a white lacquered console, a white enamel ash tray, a Gothic statue of the virgin with faded paint. Presiding over it all, a splendid Miró whose colors were all the more astonishing amid so much white.

Neus had already had three whiskeys—Neus, your photos will come out blurry—and I had consumed the entire pitcher of orange juice, natural, of course, and we were both getting impatient.

"What if she called the magazine to find out... She must know by now that we're not...." said Neus.

"Don't worry, I have everything figured out. The director is a friend of mine and he knows what to say if anyone calls."

"But when she sees that no article is coming out... "

"One will come out."

"With my photos? In *Pink and Blue?* Do you mean it, Lònia?"

She was beside herself with professional gratitude. If that calmed her down and she played her role well, few lies would have served me so well in so little time.

Although, after all, why did it have to be a lie? *Pink and Blue* published silly articles by definition. If I turned my notes over to the director, no matter how banal they were, someone at the publication would make use of them. That would be doing poor Neus a favor, since that way she could do her work for better pay.

She specialized in photographs of weddings and first communions for one of those standard companies. At night, especially during the summer, she freelanced in restaurants and cabarets, looking for people who wanted a visual reminder of their nocturnal follies. Over the hill playboys—when I was young in Majorca we called them skirt-chasers—they were real collectors —flirts; there were also middle-aged couples who allowed themselves a night out on the town once in their lives, and groups of bachelors holding wild bachelor parties... They were silly pictures but they documented the era. In any case, she kept copies filed away.

Sometimes she did freelance reports which she would try to sell to some magazine. She had never succeeded. And that business of stills from films seemed an exaggeration to me.

Having her name in print in a magazine like *Pink and Blue* wasn't exactly a great professional coup, but if I could help her get a foot in the door at least, I didn't want to be responsible for her losing the opportunity.

At that moment, none other than Mrs. Mireia Gallart Purgilòs d'Antal, Baroness of Prenafeta, made her entry. She was tall, blonde and light-complexioned, with small, cold blue eyes. She had the thinness characteristic of women who are obsessed with flab and torture themselves with brutal diets; if she had been that thin naturally, she would have tried to gain a few pounds. No one's happy the way they are. But the Baroness seemed proud of her angular body, from her drawn cheeks to her chest, flat as a board.

"I still can't imagine what interest your magazine could have in me. My husband is the important one in the family," she lied without trying to hide it.

She showed us the entire house and explained her daily activities in detail, but when it came to talking about her husband, she was evasive.

"Are those books in the white room bound in white leather to make them match?"

"Certainly not, Miss. That would be a sacrilege for an interior decorator."

That appeased me, because it seemed awfully tacky.

"As a matter of fact, the room is done in white to compliment those books, which have belonged to the family for over three hundred years."

"Is that little wooden statue on the dresser in the vestibule a real antique, too?"

"You're very observant... But what do you mean, a real antique? It's Art Nouveau... Oh, you mean is it a recent imitation? No, no, certainly not."

"Is it your husband who acquires these antiques?"

"My husband? He's not interested in antiques... That's something that has to come from your family... He couldn't tell a 19th century stone gargoyle from one of those wooden dolls the Africans sell in their little booths... Don't put that down, Miss, it would be in very bad taste and might be misinterpreted. Just put that I take care of the interior decoration, since he's so busy with his business that he doesn't have any free time to concern himself with the house."

It was a chance to ask about his business, but I took another tack.

"What are the most recent pieces you've acquired?"

"Oh, it's been about a year since any antiques have come into the house. Those things come when they come. That Romanesque capital was the last thing... No, don't photograph it, private collectors aren't supposed to have pieces like that."

"What do you mean?"

"There are people who talk about public domain and things like that. But everything I have I purchased legally, with all the papers in order. Anyway, it's better for people like us, who know how to take care of them, to have them, than to let them be ruined by the elements. That wrought-iron cross, for example, was rusting away in the cemetery of an abandoned town in the Pyrenees."

I was getting tired of taking useless notes, and I felt sorry for Neus, who would go broke taking all those pictures. So I took the bull by the horns.

"I'd like you to tell me about an ordinary day in your life. Yours and your husband's, of course, but from your point of view."

Living with an important man had its advantages, but also its drawbacks. No, they hadn't had kids, and that was too bad, but at least it allowed her to take care of the inheritance, the family name. Yes, her husband was a born businessman, and now he didn't need to do so much work, since the business went pretty much on its own, but even so . . . he didn't want anyone to say that he lived off his wife, and besides, she had lost track of the businesses he had, and she didn't know too much about business anyway. So, once again, my efforts failed.

No, he had never gotten into politics, but he talked about it often lately, and who knows, such a restless man, but he liked things to be clear, and politics is so complicated. Many of his friends were into it, but they never talked about it when they came over, among other things because he had friends in all the different parties and he wanted to avoid arguments.

Her delight at talking about her husband was too much and the image of her life was too idyllic. Still, she maintained a rather monotonous calm during my questioning, and she answered exactly as she pleased. It was only when I asked her why she had Filipinos as gardener and maid that a few wrinkles appeared around her lips.

"Why are you asking me that? What's the harm?"

The conversation became icy. She answered in monosyllables, or she told me bluntly that she didn't like the question. Finally, she threw us out. Politely, of course, without losing her composure.

"I can't spend any more time with you, I'm sorry. The visit has been delightful. Please send me a copy of the magazine, I never buy it."

"May I see that statue again?" I asked as we passed the dresser again. "It's gorgeous."

"My paternal grandfather gave it to my grandmother on their honeymoon to Paris, in 1906...."

"We could take one last photo here, Neus...."

Friday morning

"Where's the photo of the little statue?"

"I didn't have any more film, Lònia. I had been snapping without it for a while already."

"But I clearly wanted a picture of the statue... Why do you think I asked you to do it?"

Neus shrank back. Quim realized I was about to get carried away and really let her have it.

"It won't do you any good to argue now," he said.

"But that was the most important photo, the key. And this dummy... "

"Why didn't you tell me?"

"This one I want with film, Neus. Is that what I was supposed to say? And here I was worried about how much film you were wasting!"

"If that statue was so important, why didn't you have me photograph it in the beginning, when we were just nosing around?"

She was right. But I hadn't realized it at the time. And now I couldn't admit it in front of Neus and Quim.

"Did you bring me the bill?" I said to end the discussion.

I wrote her a check and shooed her away. I couldn't stand seeing her around with that hang-dog look.

"If she told you it was a gift from her grandfather it's not the antique dealer's statue," Quim said.

"How do you know she wasn't lying?"

He finally convined me not to get so worked up. To appease him, I telephoned Gaudí and went to see her with the whole file. On the way, to console myself, I bought a lipstick.

Mr. Antal was, in fact, one of the men she was looking for.

But neither of the others appeared in any of the photos I showed her.

"Where is this place?" she asked.

"It's his house. Full of antiques, good ones, it seems to me. And this is his wife."

"What did you go to the house for? I told you just to get their names and some way to contact them."

I found myself, unwittingly, giving explanations to her about how I did my job and why. It was too late; she had the upper hand.

"The more information I have about him, the easier it will be to find the other two," I said.

"What information did you get from this visit?"

I gave her the report. She glanced at it indifferently.

"I didn't ask you for this. Did you take pictures of people who work in his company?"

"Not yet. You keep calling the office, so I decided to bring you everything I had so far."

"Wouldn't it have been better to take pictures in his office than snoop around his house? I'm looking for three men, as you know."

She was most disagreeable.

"It's not that easy to do an article for a silly magazine about a businessman in his own office."

"That takes the cake! What article?"

"How did you think I could get into the house and photograph everything? Laser beams?"

Damn her!

"I'm not interested in all that, or in the photos of the house and the wife. Just like you took pictures at the company door, you could take pictures of people leaving."

"My photographer wasn't available at starting time, or quitting time. That's what I planned to do tomorrow, but since you were in such a hurry, I brought you preliminary results of my investigations."

I felt like slapping her.

"You don't need to do anything tomorrow. Maybe I already have enough. I'll speak to him, and maybe I won't need to find the other two. Send me the bill."

I hadn't said anything about the Filipino apartment, nor did I feel like telling her about the unphotographed statue. She could eat her heart out!

She gave me back all the photos except the clearest one of Mr. Antal. And even though she said she wasn't interested in the report, she kept it.

That afternoon, as pissed-off as I was, I had rabbit with garlic sauce for lunch. I hadn't eaten meat for five years. I decided I wouldn't send her a bill, and that I would take pictures everywhere—the company, the foundations he was involved in, the clients of Finesor, clubs and associations Antal had anything to do with. Thousands of photos, even if I went broke paying Neus. I would send them free of charge to Mrs. Gaudí so she could wallpaper the shop.

That evening, with garlic sauce rumbling in my stomach and rabbit hopping around in my gut, I decided Quim was right, I was crazy, Gaudí was right, I was irresponsible and inept, and that it was about time I learned my job, after having spent five years at it.

As I was touring boarding houses in the useless search for Sebastiana, the sordidness of the places I was visiting, and the dark little lives that were lived there enclosed in the shadows, attacked the rest of me that was unaffected by the garlic sauce. I only felt a little better when I got to one of the side streets off Escorial, in a new and pleasant apartment building which a lot of people used for rendezvous. At least it was air-conditioned.

It was a muggy night. From the time I fell asleep to the time I woke up, I dreamed of nothing but Filipinos.

V

Saturday morning

I'd had the people at *Pink and Blue* wrapped around my little finger ever since I let them in on the secret wedding of the daughter of the Savings Bank director. I was discreetly investigating her disappearance for the family, who feared a runaway more than a kidnapping. But suddenly rumors started appearing in the papers. The family hadn't said anything to anyone, not even the police; nor had they received any ransom demands. But now everyone was talking about kidnapping, and not for money or political reasons, but as a way of getting even with the father, whose shady deals were all beginning to surface. Then I found the girl. She had married a gypsy, naturally against the wishes of the family. That's why she had disappeared from the face of the earth. I gave the exclusive story to *Pink and Blue*, and the wedding pictures had doubled their circulation for four weeks. It earned me a press card, which often comes in handy, as well as the eternal gratitude of the director. I should also add that I would put them on the trail to some juicy story or other once in a while—the sensationalist, speculative kind—to keep that gratefulness alive.

So they not only accepted the story about the Baroness of Prenafeta, they also paid for the photos and gave Neus a contract.

"But don't give her a job for about a month. At the moment I need her to work for me exclusively."

Neus had arrived at the office a few minutes before I did, still looking guilty.

"What's this?" she asked, looking alarmed as I handed her the check from *Pink and Blue.*

"The price they paid for your photo story on the Baroness. And you can go see them whenever you want. You have a contract assured."

"This is highway robbery, Lònia!"

I was stunned. Highway robbery, she said, the hypocrite! Surely she had never earned so much in her whole life!

"I mean for them to pay me all this . . . it wasn't worth this much, either in material or for the job . . . It's as if I were cheating them, me, charging so much for so little. Where I work they don't pay me this much in six months. Besides, you already paid me!"

Quim was playing innocent. Boy scouts, the two of them.

"Look, you've had some hard times, and now you're getting your due. I couldn't pay so much, but since the magazine is generous . . . "

Neus' eyes were sparkling.

"But first you have to do a few little chores for me . . . You can give up your job right away . . . ."

I gave her a list. It wasn't necessary to find out whether Antal's relationship with all those associations was close or frequent. I wanted photos of the people who hung around there. All the people possible. Especially men.

Then I realized I didn't have any idea of the age of the two men I was looking for, or what they looked like. Really, I wasn't even half a detective.

I shook off the discouraged feeling. Men who were more or less Antal's age. Warmed-over studs, I told Neus.

Neus, delighted with her new prospects in life, accepted the job happy as could be.

"Now, let's get to work looking for Sebastiana," I said, satisfied with myself.

Quim's innocent expression became sour.

"You buy people with no scruples at all, Paloni."

I turned to stone. Here I thought I'd done a good deed and this priest's apprentice accused me of trafficking in the female photographer's slave trade.

Orient Sunshine came to mind, but I brushed it aside with a

shrug. I grabbed Saturday's newspapers. Sebastiana's letter to her parents was dated Saturday.

There were, in fact, ads that didn't appear the rest of the week. Apartment. Private house. Decent. Independence. Telephone. Terrace. Furnished.

"Yes, the girl who rented it from me just left. Maybe she'll come back in a few days, but since she didn't leave a deposit...."

It was on Valencia Street, a building typical of the Eixample neighborhood, without too many curlicues on the facade, but not too plain, either. It was pretty run down on the inside, with a long hallway that meandered in the dim light. The telephone in the entry was shared by everyone. The bathroom too.

"Oh, that Joseph, he must have just showered..." said the woman who ran the boardinghouse, who lived in the other apartment on the same floor.

"Who's Joseph?"

He was the guy in room one. The first door on the right, starting at the end of the hallway. Then there was a travelling salesman, who was hardly ever there, and then Mr. Torres, who was retired and never used the bath, only the toilet for a few minutes first thing in the morning. The bathtub would only be used by Joseph and me.

She knocked on Joseph's door and scolded him maternally for not cleaning the bathtub after using it.

The hallway hadn't been swept for years and cobwebs were hanging from the ceiling. But when she showed me the room, if I'd had balls they would have fallen on the floor. It was a dark room, lit like a purgatory scene with tulip shaped lamps, colored plastic. A formica wardrobe with two sections looked like an enormous filing cabinet and took up half the room. A headboard with a stained, lumpy mattress, two chairs that didn't match anything and a big formica shelf with one of the first televisions to hit the market. Oh, yes, with a plastic lace cover and an imitation porcelain pitcher.

The terrace was a tiny ledge. A thousand-year-old plastic curtain hid the depressing view of the narrow airwell full of soot from kitchens and the elevator. It was darker out there than inside.

The woman enthusiastically showed me the size of that wardrobe and praised the quietness of the room.

"There's no heater, for the winter," I observed.

"No, but don't worry. It's never cold in this house."

"Is there hot water in the shower?"

"No . . . "

"And you have the nerve to ask 22,000 pessetes a month for this hole, madam?"

"What do you mean?"

Perhaps Sebastiana had lived here. Or some other helpless, inexperienced girl. An old man, a travelling salesman and a student lived here and that witch was earning nearly 100,000 a month for the filthy shitty place.

I showed her the picture of Sebastiana. She got scared.

"Who are you? Didn't you come to rent an apartment?"

I stared at her, without blinking an eye. I held the photo up at eye level.

"Did she do something bad?" she stammered. "She seemed a little strange to me, sad, I would say."

"Where is she now?"

"She left yesterday. She said she might come back, but she didn't leave me a deposit, so the apartment was empty and I put the ad in again."

"She didn't say where she was going?"

"No, and I didn't ask her. I don't mind my lodgers' business. Are you from the police? Did the girl take drugs? Because I won't let her in if she comes back. I want decent people here. Who knows what we're coming to?"

"When will she be back?"

"I don't know if she'll be back . . . she said maybe . . . "

"When?"

"Maybe Monday . . . But are you with the police?"

"No, madam. But if you haven't called me by Monday to tell me she's back, I assure you you'll have the police. I'll see to it that this racket you've got going gets blown sky-high, understand?"

The shuffling of the woman's old house slippers followed me to the door apprehensively. I waited for her to open it so I wouldn't get my hands dirty. She left my card filthy when she took it.

"And don't tell her anyone is looking for her."

I flew down the two flights of stairs. I was sick to death of unscrupulous people and stupid people. For 2,000 pessetes more those lodgers could have exchanged that sordid piece of shit for a carpeted place with a kitchenette, a private telephone, a private bathroom, heat and a refrigerator. I don't know which was worse, the apartment next door being used as a flophouse or having that witch disguised as a middle-class matron for a neighbor.

I walked around the neighborhood for a good while. Saturday afternoon silence, the emptiness of closed-up shops, the mugginess of a close sky without a breeze. That desertion of the city announced the approach of July, when half the population would be away on vacation.

The idea of solitude among the crowds is bullshit. I felt alone precisely because there were no people around. There's nothing sadder than an empty city in broad daylight.

Monday morning

"I'm a friend of Jerònia. Your mother asked me to look for you."

Sebastiana was shocked. She didn't want to go back to Majorca. Couldn't her mother and Jerònia leave her alone? She wasn't sick, she was okay, she was just sick of living at home and since she was sure they wouldn't let her go, she had run away.

"Well, you don't look too good."

She burst into tears. She was pale, undone. She looked so needy that I was overwhelmed by a maternal instinct.

"Please don't tell them anything. Don't tell them you found me, please."

"Do you have a job in Barcelona? How long can you keep paying for this dump?"

"I can take care of myself."

"Where have you been these last few days?"

"With a friend."

"Who? Do you shoot up?"

She didn't know what I meant.

"You're pregnant, then."

It wasn't a question, it was an assertion that she couldn't deny. The sobs shook her whole body and she collapsed on the bed, helpless.

"I'll make a deal with you. For the moment I won't tell your family I found you. But you have to come and stay with me."

"Do you really mean it?"

I couldn't take it back now. Sebastiana started to toss things hurriedly into her suitcase. She was lucky it was me who found her. She would have accepted the same offer from anyone.

I called Mercè from the entry hall and kept the landlady from charging the girl a day's rent. Instead of going directly to my place, we would go to the doctor.

I couldn't get her to say anything on the way. When she saw *Gynecologist's Office* on the door she freaked.

"You live here?"

"No, but if you're pregnant, you should be checked, don't you think? Don't worry, she's a friend of mine and she'll be discreet."

"You tricked me! And the landlady did, too! Everybody tricks you in Barcelona!"

She started to run down the stairs. I stopped her at the door to the street and she broke down in my arms. The concierge came out to see what was going on.

"Call Mercè, the doctor on the third floor! Don't just stand there wringing your hands!"

Sebastiana was kicking my legs and punching my arms. She had me pretty bruised up by the time Mercè got downstairs. If she hadn't been such a poor wretched kid I would have let her have it with a couple of those punches Quim showed me, and she'd have been put out. But I didn't dare. Mercè didn't hesitate. Two slaps delivered with assurance and experience calmed her down immediately.

"Now, if you want to, we can leave," I said.

"She can't go like this. She needs to rest a little," Mercè diagnosed.

"But if she doesn't want you to check her we can't force her," I said in all sincerity, foolishly tormented by moral scruples. "Nor would I want to."

"Okay . . . Since you're here, I could take advantage of the opportunity to do your check-up while she's resting. I certainly don't need to oblige anybody. I have plenty of clients."

Mercè was stubborn. She hadn't even looked at Sebastiana since she had slapped her. I looked at her myself, questioningly, and she shook her head yes.

She was two months along. Because of a rape.

Sunday

It had been a relatively quiet week. Catch-up work at the office, Neus calling every day to tell me she had spent twelve hours taking pictures and twelve closed up in the laboratory—when do you sleep, honey?—and Quim had taken advantage of the calm to disappear, but not before giving me a sermon about Sebastiana, naturally.

"At least you should tell Lady Jerònia."

"Milady."

"Whatever. You're not going to change the subject. At least tell Jerònia so she can calm the parents down."

"Parents who can't even calm their own daughter down."

"What's gotten into you? The daughter didn't give them the chance."

"Why do you think she didn't? Because she was afraid. And why would she be afraid to tell her parents she had been raped? Because they would have added fuel to the fire. And if they find out she's pregnant, they'll come looking for her to give her hell, and that will be her undoing."

"What the hell has gotten into you with this kid? It's her problem, isn't it? Are you prepared to be accused of kidnapping?"

"What are you talking about?"

"If her parents find she's with you and you didn't tell them . . ."

"Don't worry about that . . . Quim, you're such a nice guy, and now you want me to do a mean thing like that!"

"I don't get you at all."

He took off, leaving me submerged in doubts and responsible for an indecisive kid. If she didn't decide soon, she'd make me a grandparent.

She didn't want to have the baby. But abortions were a sin. She had already tried it; by the time I found her she had gone with another girl she met on the street who had fixed concoctions for her to drink and massaged her, but when the time came for the shot, she got scared and came back to the pension.

"Whether you have it or not, in your situation—no need to hide it now—your parents won't take you back," I said.

For a whole week she wouldn't leave the house. She thought her condition would be obvious to everyone and they'd all bawl her out. And we spent every evening rehashing the same conversation.

If that had happened to me when I was fifteen, I wouldn't have dared to tell my parents, and I would have thought abortion was a sin, too. That's why I understood perfectly the poor kid's situation and her state of mind. What I didn't understand was that things had changed so little in twenty years.

Sooner or later I would have to tell Jerònia something.

VI

Monday morning

I left Sebastiana at Mercè's office and went to my office. Neus was waiting for me with a huge pile of photos. While we were looking at them, Jerònia showed up unexpectedly. Just when Jerònia was telling me that Sebastiana's parents had decided to turn the case over to the police, the telephone interrupted us.

"We can't publish the story on the Baroness," the director of *Pink and Blue* told me.

"Why not?"

"Because even for a shitty magazine like ours it's in very bad taste to run a story on the life and works of such a recent widow."

"What the hell?"

"Mr. Felip Antal died in the wee hours of Saturday night-Sunday morning. Don't you read the papers?"

So many questions were exploding in my head that they got all tangled up and couldn't come out.

"Nothing to say?"

"May he rest in peace. . . . Listen, what on earth did he die of? The Baroness didn't say anything about him being sick."

"He was as healthy as a clove of garlic. An accident. He ran into a wall. They say he'd been drinking."

"When's the funeral?"

"They cremated him yesterday. Nothing left but ashes. Listen, Lònia, I called to find out if you and the friend you recommended could take some photos at the funeral . . . We called the house and they don't want to have anything to do with the press,

45

but maybe since you know the Baroness... The, uh, official funeral is tomorrow... "

"Okay, we'll try."

While I was trying to make some sense out of the whirlwind churning in my head—Sebastiana, Jerònia, the cops, the Filipinos, Antal, Gaudí, the photographs and Neus—the phone rang again.

"Miss Lònia Guiu?"

"Speaking. Who's calling?"

"This is Elena Gaudí."

"What a coincidence!"

"Coincidence? Why?"

"I just read that Mr. Antal suffered a fatal accident."

"That's why I'm calling. It's no coincidence. I met with him on Thursday. He was very evasive. But today we were to meet again with his companion who has the statue, and... "

"Are you sure, Mrs. Gaudí?"

"Of what? I'm sure we had an appointment today and that the appointment has been cancelled."

"I mean are you sure the guy you had an appointment with has the statue?"

"Why do you ask?"

"In any case, why don't you go to the meeting anyway? Maybe the guy will show up with the statue and everything. Not the dead one, of course, the other one."

"Miss Guiu, you know as well as I do that he won't show up. Especially now, after the, uh, accident," she pronounced the last word syllable by syllable.

"Are you saying it wasn't an accident?"

"What do you think? I don't know, and I don't care. But I think the funeral would be a good place to find the two men who were with him when he came to my shop."

"Mrs. Gaudí, I'm way ahead of you. The magazine Pink and Blue just asked me to do a report on that very funeral."

"What are you, a journalist or a detective?"

"Both, and a lot more besides. Suspicious, for one thing. I'm not sure it's necessary to take all those pictures."

"What do you mean? Why not?"

46

"You're the one who called, so I assume that means you're hiring me again, right?"

"Of course."

"Fine. But I've been working for you for free this whole week, and before I go on I have something I'd like to show you. I'll be at your shop in an hour."

I hung up without giving her a chance to say no. I closed my eyes for a minute and then I told Jerònia to stop the report to the police immediately, since I was hot on Sebastiana's trail and if the police got involved it would spoil everything. I would have her in twenty-four hours. I told her not to leave Barcelona and to give me a telephone number where I could reach her.

Then I asked Neus if she had grouped the photographs according to the place she had taken them.

"Just like you told me."

"Good girl. Grab them and let's go. I'll explain on the way."

I couldn't call Mercè in front of Jerònia. So the three of us left the office together and when we separated I called her from a booth.

"Have the girl wait for me at your place. No matter how late. Tell her Jerònia is in Barcelona but I haven't told her that I found her, only that I'm on the trail. Okay?"

"I'm sorry to tell you, Miss Guiu, that you've done all this work for nothing . . . "

That Gaudí was stiff as a corpse. Maybe from dealing with so many lifeless objects.

She had been looking at the photos with great interest. She almost seemed troubled, but she was incapable of expressing any emotion except coldness. She did think it was a good way to find the two men she was still looking for. She told me that even though she had terminated my services, she would pay me for the work I had done that week on my own, at my own risk.

But when she saw that the two men weren't among the people in the photos, the crumbs of goodwill toward me began to dissolve.

I got pissed-off.

"And I'm sorry to tell you, Mrs. Gaudí, that I don't believe a word of what you've told me. I don't believe there was ever a falsified check, because Mr. Antal had plenty of money to pay for an antique no matter how expensive it was. I don't believe the other two men exist. In any case, the only thing I believe is that the statue exists, because I saw it with my very own eyes, precisely, in Mr. Antal's house."

It was her eyes that popped out now. I had trapped her. I had her between a rock and a hard place, and I kept on squeezing.

"You got mad because I went to Antal's house, and even though you wanted me to look for three men, you cut me off when I had found one. Either you didn't want me snooping around certain places, or the other two don't exist. And now, the only one who showed any signs of life can't show them any more. That's when you called me, wanting me to start looking again. I'm sorry to tell you, dear Mrs. Gaudí, but the whole thing smells like a rat. What are you trying to do? Tie my hands by giving me a contract? Get me off the trail so I won't tell anyone? I'm warning you that if you don't give me a plausible explanation, if my questions don't get satisfactory answers, you'll not only have to do without my services, you'll have to deal with the police."

My voice resounded among the antiques in the shop in shadows. I wonder if antique shops are always shadowy for atmosphere or to hide the flaws in the old pieces?

When the echo of my threat had died down, only a stoney silence remained. I waited a few seconds, during which the objects hidden in the crowded shadows seemed ready to attack me. Before anything could happen though, I started to talk again. Like when I was a kid and I would start to sing when I was afraid of the dark . . .

"For example, I'd like to know . . . "

"Look, Miss Guiu," she interrupted me. "I . . . I'll tell you the truth."

She was giving up the ship. I began to listen.

" . . . and I hope you'll understand, and above all, that I can keep counting on you. Frankly, both my personal and professional prestige are involved. Anybody can make a mistake; I won't deny that I thought I was making a terrific deal, and my

48

own greed caught up with me. If you don't help me, you won't need to go to the police, because a colleague of mine will turn me in...." She paused a little longer this time, and her voice was becoming a hoarse whisper. "And it will be all over, everything, the store, and all that it has cost me to make a name for myself in the world of antiques... everything. It isn't the time in prison that worries me... it won't be much... but afterwards, afterwards...."

I was fascinated. I noticed that the woman was beginning to let her guard down which made me feel a little sympathy for her. But I stiffened up:

"Not so fast, madam, you might trip. And don't get off the track."

She looked at me, taken aback by my tone of voice, and because she wasn't sure she understood what I'd said.

"One step at a time, Mrs. Gaudí. Tell me what the relationship is between you and those men... or between you and Antal, and why you're looking for them."

"It's true there wasn't any bad check," she began.

I smiled from ear to ear.

"Nor is there a statue."

The smile froze on me. As if someone had hit me on the head with a hammer, or the movie had stopped short.

"It's actually a painting, a Gothic triptych from the Burgundy school. They offered it to me and I could tell they were in a hurry to sell it. I suspected it was a phony because I made them an offer and they accepted it without even trying to bargain. I knew from my experience that if it was false, it was a very good copy; it was worth taking advantage of the situation instead of wasting time with experts, since if it was a phony I could still sell it for the real thing easily. Even so, I copied their information in my register. And it's true that their names as well as their identification documents were false... The next day I had the triptych examined. It was real, a priceless original. The expert warned me that it might have been stolen. I gave him a substantial tip. A few days later I let it go to a colleague who had a possible buyer, naturally not revealing the suspicions of the expert who had certified its authenticity. Once the transaction had been made, we got a notice from the Department of Fine Arts about the disappearance of the triptych from a private French museum. My colleague came to see me with the notice and threatened to turn me into the Department for complicity. If the client found out it was stolen, and it was very likely that he would because he hobnobbed with collectors from all over the world, my colleague would be turned in too. And he didn't want to ruin his reputation."

"Who is your colleague and who's the client? And the expert?"

"I can't tell you that, Miss Guiu. It's a professional secret. Surely you understand."

"Does your colleague think you're involved in the robbery?"

"He did at first. I gave him the information from my register and that's when we discovered it was false. He realized then that I hadn't stolen it, but it didn't matter: I had committed a great crime of negligence and was an accomplice for not having investigated the sellers' credentials. And even more so for not explaining to him what the situation really was. He had accepted an object from me because of his confidence in my professionalism. On the other hand, he had only asked me for the certificate of authenticity for his client and we had agreed to leave the other paperwork of registration and ownership for another day."

"But it's possible that the buyer of the triptych won't ever find out it was stolen . . . then you won't be in any trouble."

"It's possible but not likely. Anyway, my colleague is so angry he might turn me in anyway. After the notice from the Department, anyone who knows anything about the triptych and doesn't speak up is also an accomplice."

"What will you do if I find the other two?"

"I'll make a statement to the Department myself."

"But you'll still be in danger of being charged as an accomplice."

"At least I'll have the advantage of having acted in good faith . . . If I have the real information about the sellers, no one will know I committed the crime of buying from them without having checked their credentials."

"But in that case, wouldn't your colleague say something?"

"I think I can make it up to him somehow. When he sees he's cleared of any charges, I think he'll calm down."

It seemed believable enough, but I still didn't believe her. Why would Antal get involved in smuggling objets d'art when he had more than enough money to get things legally? And even if he was a smuggler, why would he risk selling something in person? And especially, that accident . . .

But I didn't want to ruffle Gaudí. Now I could keep on investigating the Filipinos with the antique dealer paying me for it. Besides, I wanted to know what was going on between them and now I had an excuse to really snoop around. And besides that, I didn't have any other clients in sight.

When I went outside I realized it had been cool in the shop. That street wasn't one of the really hot ones in Barcelona because there wasn't much sun, but the air didn't circulate much either. Narrow, unpaved streets, fortunately without traffic. Even with the heat, walking there was better than on the wide avenues, stinking with smoke and crowds.

I started to see a few tourists, unmistakable in their ridiculous costumes. The Cathedral Plaza was full of tour buses and the traffic was blocked up.

I called Mercè from a booth. She was home with Sebastiana. I would go get her as soon as I ate.

I called Jerònia, and then I went back to the pedestrian zone in the Gothic quarter and walked to the vegetarian restaurant on Portaferrissa Street.

Slowly, without pushing, I tried to convince Jerònia, over an extravagant and delightful salad, to leave the girl alone for a while.

Jerònia's hair stood on end when I told her Sebastiana was pregnant. At first she refused to believe it was because of a rape. She finally came around and seemed ready to accept my advice, but she was sure the parents . . . But that's what social workers were for, right? To solve conflicts like this? Did she want to make Sebastiana unhappy? She should prepare the parents in case Sebastiana wanted an abortion. Jerònia freaked out when she heard me utter the terrible word. No way!

I tried to make her understand that if Sebastiana decided to do that, everything would be easier for everybody. The tragedy could be covered up. On the other hand, the poor kid would have to live the rest of her life with a skeleton in her closet, while the rapist would go on living in peace without anyone bothering to hunt him down, I thought aloud with words taken from the mouth of Mercè.

"Who, uh, raped her?" Jerònia asked in a whisper.

"She doesn't know. She didn't know him, she says . . . It was a group of guys. If charges were pressed, it wouldn't be hard to track him down."

But Jerònia said it would be useless, and besides it would cause a scandal the parents wouldn't be able to deal with.

And if they did keep the rape and abortion quiet, instead of reporting it, I'd have to keep that cover-up from Mercè. Because if she found out that I had cooperated in letting the perpetrators go unpunished I would lose her friendship forever. She was very strict about politically correct feminist behavior.

Monday evening

"Do you think this is some kind of sport and I'm the manager?" Mercè was furious.

She had gotten involved in a stupid argument with Jerònia. Stupid on Jerònia's part, who insinuated that our influence— mine and Mercè's—would make the kid have an abortion against her will.

"Her will!" screamed Mercè. "A will governed by the idea of sin and punishment isn't her will, it belongs to her parents and people like you, not her!'

The quarrel lasted until Jerònia left for the airport. Sebastiana and I stayed in Barcelona with our heads spinning. Sebastiana, because she found herself between the fire and the frying pan, between two completely different concepts of liberty; me, because I had my thoughts elsewhere.

I spent the night looking at the newspapers and taking notes on the information about Antal's accident. Everything seemed so normal, within the boundaries of the misfortune. Not a single insinuation or innuendo.

VII

Tuesday morning

Gaudí showed up in disguise. It hadn't been easy to convince her that we'd make a lot more progress with her help, but after the points I'd scored yesterday, she couldn't refuse.

If she could identify the men for me directly, I could follow them right away and find out where they lived. I thought of Quim and cursed him. I could only follow one man by myself, and who knows where he was, probably off scratching his belly somewhere. On the other hand, as I kept telling Gaudí, if I had to depend on the photos, I would have to go through other people to find a thread that would connect the image of the person with the name and address . . .

"But you could have done that with last week's photos," she said, still unwilling.

"I had a concrete point of reference—the place they were taken. If you had told me that's the guy, I could have started to look among the members of that association or club. Just by showing the picture to a waiter or a doorman I would have found the thread . . . On the other hand, at a funeral, to find out the identity of one of the people who shows up means an extremely complicated investigation . . . and a dangerous one." Anyway, I had Neus come with us, since Quim wasn't around.

I left the car in front of the church. There wasn't a bar on that stretch of the street. There were lots of official cars, though, some with a Catalan flag and others with a Spanish flag. There were some private cars, too, with chauffeurs, and lots of women dressed in black—you couldn't tell whether they were going to an evening ball or a funeral. There were so many arrangements and bouquets of flowers that you couldn't breathe the air in that whole block.

I had a little contretemps with a traffic cop who tried to throw me out. Even my press card had no effect on him. But I had parked in a space that wasn't marked, alongside other parked cars, so if he wanted me to move, he would have to send for a tow truck. I was doing my job and the Constitution gave me every right to do so as long as I didn't break any laws, I told him solemnly.

"How much do these fat cats bribe you to keep the street empty?" My tone was much less solemn now.

The man was stubborn, but I was even more so. I ceremoniously took out a little notebook and asked him for his identification number. Naturally, he laughed and refused to give me either his name or his number. But he let me stay parked where I was: he had seen Neus with the camera and he didn't like the idea of being photographed at all.

I wondered when the day would come that all guards and policemen would wear their identification on their lapels. Then they'd really have to mind their p's and q's.

People started to go into the church and the street was clearing out. You could hear organ music from inside, and the smell of incense overpowered the flowers for a few moments.

It was Saint Mary's month, and the chapel was full of girls. We still wore white uniforms with starched collars in those days. Sister Magdalena played the harmonium—you could hear the pedals more than the music. Sister Francisca was slowly scattering incense and Sister Catalina directed the final song. Salve Reginaaaaaa! The odor of the flowers, the wax and the smoke; the trembling of the candles and the buzz of the harmonium; my knees were aching from the straw mats that dug into your skin; religious emotion . . . All in all, it made me pass out and they had to carry me to the patio. When I came to, they sent me home. When I undressed to turn in, I realized it was my first period.

If someone had told me then that that memory would come to me when I was working as a detective in Barcelona, I wouldn't have known what they were talking about.

But now I had to jump out of the car quickly, the memory abruptly cut off.

"That's him! That's him," Elena Gaudí was saying in an intense and urgent tone.

Neus was shooting like crazy.

The man was getting out of a taxi that had stopped between the church door and us.

Shit, a taxi! I got in and the taxi started up. When the driver asked me where to, I handed him a bill and asked him where he picked up that passenger. The driver wouldn't talk. I showed him another bill. Nothing. Finally I told him to take me back to the place he picked me up.

"Why do you want to know?" He asked before I got out.

"He's my husband. He's having an affair, and I want to know with whom, and where. He told me the funeral was at ten, and it's past twelve . . . "

The taxi driver told me not to worry about that stuff, that boys will be boys, but they always come back home . . .

"What would you do if your wife was having an affair?"

"Oh, that's different!"

"Are you going to tell me, or not?"

"On the corner of Urgell and Gran Via. The Mar-Llobregat side."

He didn't want to accept more than what the meter said, but I thanked him and gave him a tip that tripled the fare.

The information might be a good starting place, or it could be a wild goose chase. But it was better than a kick in the ass.

I went back to my car.

Time passed slowly. The funeral was high-rent—one o'clock came and went, and still it went on. The sun was starting to hit where we were, making the heat unbearable.

I moved the car from its parking space and parked on the other side, beyond the church. But as I crossed the street I saw him coming.

He and Carvalho had been in a corner, looking at everything and everyone with menacing eyes. When I came up with two glasses of

champagne, he said that the lukewarm semi-sec tasted like horse piss.
"I've never tried it myself," I said.
Carvalho tried a smile, but it looked more like he was making a
face. He didn't move a muscle.
I drank both glasses in front of them, to their health, and walked
away. Who did they think they were? If they didn't like their colleagues, why did they come to the meetings?
As a matter of fact, I wasn't enjoying myself at all either. But I
didn't consider myself superior to the others, and it bothered me that
they looked at me with arched brows.
I left promptly, and as I was getting into the elevator, Arquer came
up beside me.* He insisted I have dinner with him. I took him to a
vegetarian restaurant, and he told me he liked imaginative cooking,
whether it had meat or not. He told me he was shy, and that's why he
put up a shell. I didn't believe him, but I didn't argue.
I hadn't seen him again until now.

He shuffled up slowly, crossed the street and entered the
church. The biggest fish in the business. No, I wasn't mistaken,
it was him. What in the world was he doing at the funeral? An
old hunting dog like Arquer meant there was a stray lamb somewhere.

I waited a minute and went into the church myself to make
absolutely sure I was right. It was hotter inside than out, even
though the fans were going full speed. The darkness blinded me
momentarily, and I leaned against a pillar until my eyes adjusted
to the candlelight. Then I looked around for him. I had to be
careful. If he saw me, he would wonder the same thing I was
wondering. But I had an advantage over him: I remembered him
perfectly, and he might not remember me at all. Even so, I was
careful. I confirmed his identity without him even suspecting
that I was sniffing around.

I slipped out of the church. It would have been great if I could
talk to him and find out a few things. But it was too risky. He
was better at sniffing around than I was.

* Lluís Arquer is a well-known ficticious freelance detective created by Catalan
writer Jaume Fuster; Pepe Carvalho is a similar character created by Manuel
Vásquez Montalbán.

56

People started to leave. Keep your eyes peeled, I said to myself, and did.

Our man came out, with a group of other people. He chatted with a couple of people, and Gaudí peered out from behind her dark glasses, not saying anything about seeing the third man. I had the car ready to take off when I needed to, and Neus was taking pictures with the telephoto lens.

The other cars formed a damn traffic jam right in front of the church. If it didn't clear up, I risked losing sight of him, and then I would have to pick up the trail the taxi driver had given me.

But once in a while it happens that good luck comes my way, and this was one of those occasions.

A few people and a few cars began to escape from the crowd. Two men and a woman were coming towards us, and one of them was the one Gaudí had recognized. Neus took advantage getting close-up shots, while Gaudí crouched down in the back seat.

They passed us, and got into a car parked a little ways beyond ours. When they left, I was right behind them.

The day we followed Antal, Neus had been scared, but she had taken it all stoically. Now she didn't seem to mind. The one who got really bent out of shape was the antique dealer.

As I ran all the red lights all the way down Muntaner, the woman gripped the back of my seat and screamed like a lunatic. Stop, stop, if you don't let me out I'm going to jump! She didn't seem the same woman who had hired me—dry, august, distant. I saw her framed in the rear view mirror, frantic.

Neus kept telling her, but don't you see, we'll lose him now that we've found him; that she'd been about to shit in her pants the first time too, but that Lònia knew a thing or two about driving, and there wasn't any danger . . . just at that moment I had to swerve to the left to avoid an oncoming car, who had the green light, after all. The dark glasses Gaudí was hiding behind fell off from the jolt.

From the corner of my eye I could see she was looking for the handle to open the door. Neus screamed, don't open it! I cursed and told her to hold on. I changed lanes suddenly and there was a deafening screech. I pulled over to the curb.

"Get out quick so we can keep on going."

Neus could barely get the back door closed while the car was racing ahead again. But it was too late. In the heavy traffic on Muntaner, I couldn't see a sign of the car. But I didn't give up. I slowed down at each intersection. Nothing. Nothing at all.

On Mallorca Street I thought I saw him, and I made a left from the right lane. The guy in one lane had time to slam on his brakes, but not the guy in the other lane. Good thing Gaudí wasn't in the back seat. The impact would have flattened her.

Anyone who hasn't had an accident in Barcelona doesn't know what a pain it is. And if the driver is a woman, it's even worse. I was suddenly surrounded by screaming men who were siding with the driver who ran into me. When people yell at me, I either start crying or yell louder. And I did plenty of yelling that day, but out of rage. I had never lost a car before, and I lost it because of the very person I was following it for.

Someone once told me to beware if you've had good luck; it means some bad luck is coming. I'd had mine.

It was after I'd filled out all the insurance forms, and the stream of traffic returned to its normal flow down Muntaner, and the men had gotten tired of practicing the sport of yelling stupid insults, that I heard Neus telling me not to worry, that she remembered the license number perfectly. I did too.

Curiously, I had the same bit of information that had led me to Antal, plus some photos. So much work for a few crumbs!

Tuesday evening

I couldn't do anything with the car registration until the next morning, so I thought I'd try my luck with the lead the taxi driver had given me. But I got nowhere. I looked at all the mail-boxes at the corner but they were all private apartments. The doorman thought I was crazy when I described the man and asked if he lived there. What did I want him for? Why didn't I tell him the man's name, and then he could help me? No one of that description and age lived there, he finally told me. Unless he was visiting the girls on the third floor. . . .

I let it go, for the moment. If the license number didn't work out, I'd come back and search every single apartment building.

And I took Sebastiana out for a walk, acting as mother, friend, psychiatrist and counselor.

"When I was your age I would have been glad to have someone tell me what to do. But now I'm thirty-five and I can't put myself in your place."

"But what would you do? What would you do now if this happened to you?

I hesitated. I was scared to advise her. I didn't want to influence her. I didn't want to bear any responsibility for her decision, but I couldn't leave her unprotected, either. So I played Dear Abby and spoke to her sincerely and truthfully.

"To begin with, I'd press charges and try to find the rapist. Then maybe I'd decide to have the child, since I don't owe explanations to parents or family or anyone... Plus I have a business that would allow me to raise it with no problem, and at my age I don't care about people gossiping... Besides, in a city this big, no one minds your business. But on the other hand, surely I'd decide not to have it, because I didn't do it for my own pleasure, I was forced. And a child would sure change my lifestyle. I'd put myself in Mercè's hands and...."

"Wouldn't you feel bad about the kid?"

"Maybe I would. No woman wants to have an abortion. Those things aren't done for pleasure, but it would bother me more for myself than for the child... "

"It's a sin. Even though Mercè says it's not me who committed the sin. And Jerònia says I'd feel guilty all my life."

"I told you I wouldn't be a good model. I don't have any hangups about sins and guilt."

"On the other hand, maybe my parents wouldn't let me have it. And if it was them who didn't want it and they made me miscarry, it wouldn't be my fault, right?"

"I wouldn't let my parents make that decision, Sebastiana."

"No, of course, but.... "

We had arrived at Santa Maria del Mar. Sebastiana was quiet, absorbed in her tangled thoughts. I tried to leave that conflict behind, looking at the row of tall, thin, smooth columns that reminded me of the cathedral in Palma. When I first came to Barcelona and was still homesick, I would go to the breakwater to look at the sea, or come to Santa Maria. It had been about two years now since I'd seen the greasy port or the spires of the church even from a distance.

"Jerònia says I shouldn't have an abortion. If only I had a job like you, if only I lived in Barcelona... "

"Jerònia tells us not to give you advice but then she does it herself!"

I was fed up: here I was trying to be so careful not to intervene or influence, but other people didn't mind doing it. And this poor kid between a rock and a hard spot. I set my scruples aside.

"Look, Sebastiana, in your situation, I think it would be better not to have the kid. You're very young, you'll be tied down forever, always dependent on the child and on your parents. You'll never be able to lead your own life. Do you want to have it?"

"No, not really," she said, ashamed.

"Well?"

She seemed to calm down. While we had almond nectar on Argenteria Street, she decided she would go see Mercè tomorrow.

"I won't be able to go with you," I said.

"That's okay. Mercè is my friend too, now."

Wednesday morning

"I'm not going to keep the appointment with Mercè," she said instead of good morning, in a rebellious tone, as if she were disobeying an order I'd given her.

"You're not? Okay, that's fine."

"I don't want to have an abortion."

"I think that's great if that's your decision."

"You're not mad?"

"Me? Why would I be mad, honey? It's not my problem. Do whatever you want."

"Can I still stay with you?"

Shit! Playing mother, for a while, okay, but grandmother too?

"What about your parents?"

"We won't tell them anything. Jerònia promised me she wouldn't tell them anything, yet... ."

I could see myself with infuriated parents on my hands, who

would show up and rake me over the coals. But if I said no to her now, she would probably think I had some interest in her having an abortion.

"Okay. But I have to go now. I have a heavy day...."

The same bureaucrat I had dealt with trying to track down Antal was at the window. He was too familiar with me. He spoke to me in a tone of voice he wouldn't dare use with a male colleague. I knew Mercè was right, and also that before I'd heard her sermons, I hadn't noticed those differences and I'd lived much more calmly.

The car was from La Garriga, registered to Antoni Bachs, on Bisbe Street. I gave the guy a tip, but didn't return his smile.

Neus was waiting for me at the office with the photos. I just took two and I kept the ones with Bachs. Neus took the others to *Pink and Blue*.

I headed for Vallès County, going out the Meridiana. I figured I could be back in Barcelona for lunch. I figured wrong; there was a traffic jam on Meridiana.

I listened to various radio programs. I catalogued seven or eight different ways to pick one's nose, several different degrees of pleasure from head scratching and ear poking. I even had time to feel sorry for the people who lived in apartments on that beltway, and got chills wondering what would happen to someone trapped in an emergency in an ambulance in that traffic jam. Just when I was beginning to feel claustrophobic, the traffic started moving.

But by the time I got to Bisbe Street, the jewelry store was closed.* There was a vegetarian restaurant there, but it was closed, too. I bought myself a cheese sandwich and a few apricots and concentrated on being patient.

I went back to Bisbe Street at four. The woman who waited on me was the one who had accompanied the two men at the funeral. She showed me a few bracelets, which I looked at very carefully to give myself more time. Then another client came in,

---

* *Most stores and businesses still observe the siesta schedule and are open from 10 a.m. to 1 or 2 p.m. and from 4 or 5 p.m. to 8 p.m.*

and she called out for Antoni to come help her from the back of the store. Antoni wasn't the man I was looking for, he was the other one.

"Your brother showed me some plainer bracelets a few days ago," I said to the lady.

"I don't have any brothers, Miss."

"Well, your brother-in-law, then, or employee, I don't know. Some man . . . "

"Antoni, did you show this lady some bracelets a few days ago?"

Naturally, Antoni said no. The lady told me I must be thinking of another jewelry store because only she and her husband worked there, and they didn't have any other bracelets than the ones she had shown me.

I acted like I couldn't decide between two styles. Now I couldn't take the photo out of my purse and ask who the man was. So I told her I couldn't make up my mind, and thanks a lot and sorry, and I left with my tail between my legs, cursing my bones.

I did show the photo at the neighborhood bar. He might live in the neighborhood. But no. They didn't know him at all at the bar. The waiter looked at me mockingly.

He might not even be from that town. But since I'd made the trip, and had a sandwich for lunch besides, I might as well take advantage of the energy I'd spent and look a little more. But how?

If you're looking for a bully you can go from bar to bar showing his photo and it's okay. At the most someone tells him and he disappears, or they might even beat you up. If you have a name, you can ask where someone lives and nobody suspects anything and they don't even ask you what you want to know for. But the man in the picture wasn't a bully, nor did I know his name. So I didn't get anywhere showing the photo or asking where he lived.

The worst of it was that that was my last lead. They were already suspicious at Bachs' jewelry store . . . Then I had a brilliant idea. He could be a colleague. Another jewelry store.

I wasted more than an hour checking out all the jewelry stores in La Garriga in vain. One of them had a kid who I thought looked like him. I even risked showing him the picture. Nothing.

As a last resort, I went up to a local policeman and showed him the photo and my press card. I was desperate.

"No, I don't know him. What's his name? Maybe they could look it up for you at city hall, if you had his name."

Of course, don't you think I'd have gone there right away if I had his fucking name? I made up a name to get out of the mess, knowing I was getting in deeper all the time. He insisted on going with me to city hall, which was closed, but if he went along maybe they would take care of me. . . .

Sometimes an excess of helpfulness is worse than a lack of it; it's certainly harder to get away from. And just as useless. No one at city hall recognized the man in the picture, and a young kid who took it upon himself to go look it up in the register came back with nothing.

I felt stupid, but relieved when I finally gathered my photos which were being passed around the room.

I took off from city hall like a shot. Convinced that I was looking for a needle in a haystack, I got in the car and headed for Barcelona.

I was just about to get on the freeway when I made a U-turn; I would go back to Bachs' jewelry store and show them the photo. If I got into trouble, I'd get out as best I could.

On the way back to the town center, I slammed on my brakes. I had caught sight of the local magazine's sign on a balcony. Among colleagues. . . .

The people at the magazine were nice enough, but they were condescending to me.

"I'm doing a story on antique collectors, and they told me this man is a collector."

"Gòmara a collector!" one of the girls said when she saw the picture. "That's a laugh!"

"He isn't, then?"

"He only collects cash . . . ."

"Maybe if you could tell me a little about him, I won't put my foot in my mouth. I'm a beginner, and . . . " I said, humbly.

"Doesn't *Pink and Blue* have a press file?" said a good looking guy with a malicious expression.

"That's what you think? There you get by as best you can, and if you don't take care of yourself . . . "

"But with the circulation they have . . . "

"Yeah, sure, but . . . are you going to help me, or not?"

VIII

Thursday evening

The setting sun was still keeping things warm, but the air that came into the car was pleasant after a day like today.

When I turned at the fork in the road like the people at the magazine said, the sun stopped blinding me. The road leading to the factory was lined with trees, so I couldn't see the parallel road. A car emerged from it suddenly, making me slam on my brakes.

The car was blocking my way. When I got out to see what was going on, two men in uniform with pistols on their hips got out. They came up to me, looking grim. One was Filipino, or at least Asian.

"What do you want with the boss?" asked the other one, young and chubby.

"What boss? What do you mean?"

"Don't play dumb, kiddo. You've been showing his picture around to half the town and now you're asking what boss? What do you want with him?"

Who had told on me? Who had ratted? The people at city hall, at the bar, the kid at the jewelry store, the guys at the magazine? I had no way out. The road didn't lead anywhere except to the factory and to Gòmara's house next to it, camouflaged amid tropical lushness.

"Are you referring to Mr. Ernest Gòmara?" I said.

Now there was one on each side; the Catalan had grabbed my right arm and the Filipino did the same with my left, but he wasn't holding as tightly as the Catalan.

"That's what you're going to tell me. And if you don't do it quick. . . ." There was no circulation in my right hand.

"I represent the Orient Sunshine Agency. . . "

"What do you mean?"

They started to search me, leaving my hands free. I put up with it while they searched me as if I were a man. But when the fat guy's hands started playing freely with certain parts of my body, I let loose with a slap that caught him off guard, so much that instead of reaching for his gun, he grabbed me, furious.

"Grab her arms! Grab her arms!" he screamed at the Filipino, enraged, while I kept showering his face with punches. "We'll see how this prude's going to squirm with pleasure in a little while."

When he ripped my blouse and bra off, I took Quim's advice. I would aim for the weak place: a deft caress or a well-delivered blow, depending on the occasion and the opportunity, and you had them in your hands. And Quim had shown me how to do it: the knee. He hadn't needed to show me anything about caresses.

The guy had a hand on each tit, and that left him defenseless below. Leaning against the Filipino, I penetrated his boneless parts with both knees, and my boobs were set free immediately. He curled up a couple of paces away, groaning like a stuck pig.

But the Filipino didn't loosen his hold, keeping my arms behind my back. Why neither of them used their guns is still a mystery to me, unless they were inexperienced or the guns were just a decoration. The fact is that if a gun were pointing at me, I would have spread my legs without resistance. But now my hands were relatively free, at about the right place for the Filipino. Close enough to carry out the first part of Quim's advice. The little fellow shuddered and I noticed that his hands loosened.

I jerked myself away from him and turned around, blasting him in the neck with both hands. As he hit the deck, the Catalan was getting up. My hands wouldn't have been enough for him, so I used my foot. A mule kick in the head stunned him.

I ran to my car and jumped in, zigzagging towards the house; blowing the horn like an ambulance. The gates to the grounds were open. Two men in the same uniform rushed out to try to close them when they saw that the car wasn't the one they were expecting, but I floored it and didn't give them time. My car whizzed by, knocking them out of commission; one ended up in an oleander in bloom, the other against a little artificial stone fountain, dazed.

I didn't stop until I got to the main door of the house. I heard shots behind me and stayed crouched in the car until they stopped and I heard barking. Two Great Danes rushed towards me ferociously as I opened the door, but I've never been afraid of dogs and they can tell. They let me out of the car as if I were Daniel of the Old Testament and they were the lions.

The door was open, and the man I was looking for was standing at the threshold. Behind me were three more security guards, without caps but with their guns out. The two turkeys who had tried to stop me were driving in alongside the garden fence. That jerk had quite a regiment of gendarmes!

And there I was in the middle, the dogs wanting to be petted and me with my boobs hanging out.

"That's a fine way for your employees to greet people, Mr. Gòmara."

I don't know where I got the insolent tone of voice or the words. I started to cover up my breasts with what was left of my blouse, but I stopped myself.

"Come in," the man said, gesturing to his armed bulldog. The other dogs followed me amiably into the house, though.

A maid, who wasn't Filipino for a change, went to get me a robe so I could cover myself up.

"Who are you? What do you want?" Gòmara asked.

"Lònia Guiu, at your service. I don't want anything. It must be you who wants something, Mr. Gòmara. They sent me here from the Orient Sunshine Employment Agency."

"I don't know any such agency. There must be some mistake, Lònia."

It was weird that he was so nice. I was suspicious.

"Are you sure?"

The uniformed Catalan who had attacked me rushed in with my purse in one hand and my detective license in the other. Gòmara looked at the card with a grimace. I tried to make out the words on the Catalan guy's badge.

When Gòmara spoke to me again, his voice was just as sweet.

"Is this Orient, or whatever, an employment agency or a detective agency? "

"You should know that better than I do," I had decided to play hardball.

Then Gòmara, without losing his composure, searched my purse thoroughly.

"I don't like guessing games, Miss. Tell me what you're looking for here, and tell me straight. It'll be a lot better for you than if we have to force it out of you," and he smiled softly as if he were paying me a compliment instead of threatening me.

He distractedly put my card up to his ear in a gesture I wouldn't have noticed, or, if I had, I would have thought his ear itched and he was going to scratch it. Except that the two Great Danes began to growl. I looked at them and they bared their teeth. They were watching me, tense, and I felt my adrenalin level rise. The back of my neck stiffened, which dogs notice, too. It was the signal they were waiting for to attack me. I screamed—more adrenalin.

But fortunately, Gòmara's yell was louder than mine.

"Shush," and the two beasts stopped short, their bared eye teeth an inch from my thighs.

My fear made them tremble with excitement. They weren't sniffing any more; the hair on the back of their necks was standing up straight out of rage. I felt sorry for the poor things, trained this way, in contrast to their pacific nature, which you could still see in the tender looks in their humid and placid eyes.

They must have understood my feelings, because they hung their heads and moved away a few paces with their tails between their legs.

"Are you scared of dogs?" Gòmara's voice was mocking. But he didn't wait for me to answer. Returning to his mellifluous voice: "You look tired. Maybe if you rest a bit you'll get your memory back and you'll remember why you came here."

He raised his eyebrows at the creep, who grabbed me by the arm and started to pull.

"Martí, be nice to ladies!" Gòmara said.

Now his voice and expression were sarcastic and ominous.

The clock chimed... Holy Christ! the same hour that I'd turned up the street towards the factory. But the next day! Was it possible that many hours had gone by? Stretched out a whole night and the next day on the floor, without having budged from the place and position I'd fallen in as a result of Martí's amiability. While he was leading me down a hallway and then up some stairs, holding my arm tightly, I had worried about another sexual attack. The boss's cruel irony seemed like a clear go-ahead. He could do whatever he wanted to me with total impunity. If I let him.

He opened a door and there was a bed inside waiting for us. You'll have to bolt me down, I said to myself, and just as I was getting ready to prevent that, a shove and a blow on the neck made me stumble towards the bed and fall, unconscious by the time I landed. I had just a second to think—one fleeting, foggy thought—that he wouldn't need to bolt me.

I got up, not knowing what hurt the most, my bones, frozen from sleeping on the cold floor or my head full of sawdust from sleeping so long. I looked at my clothes underneath the robe: my zipper was still fastened, not broken. None of the buttons on the robe were undone. There had only been the shove and the blow to my neck.

But what was I doing in that room, with the light on, my eyes burning like porcupine quills?

The bed was a temptation I resisted valiantly, rolling over on my back, a move that brought the porcupine quills to the nape of my neck, or a little bit higher. My eyes started watering with pain as my hand palpated an enormous lump, like the one I'd gotten when I was seven, the day before first communion. I'd had a rock fight with Joana because she said that my mother had bribed the nuns so I could be in the first row for communion, and in fact it had been her mother who had tried to bribe them, and I was in the first line because I deserved it, for having memorized the catechism...

I saw myself in the mirror, like a dummy struck by the nostalgic memory. But it wasn't a first communion any more.

Nor were the metallic sounds I heard coming through the window the church bells of my home town.

The room must be in the back part of the house, where there

was a downhill slope. I found myself at the level of the second floor, and in the garden below I could see two men meticulously searching my car. They had taken the seats out and smashed them. It all looked so sad, in the dim light of the sunset. What the hell were they looking for?

I didn't have much time to lament the loss of my car. The key turned in the keyhole, and Marti the Catalan looked in. He had small malicious eyes.

"Well, have you gotten your memory back?"

He came in and locked the door from inside.

"What the hell did you hit me with, you pig?"

"I can see you haven't. I'll have to help you."

He put the key in his shirt pocket and came towards me with his arms arched along his body. His eyes had gotten even smaller.

"I can see you still haven't learned your lesson," I said.

In spite of my aching bones, sore muscles, and the porcupine quills in my head, all my senses were on alert. When he reached his arm out towards me, I grabbed it suddenly and twisted it mercilessly.

He let out a hoarse squeal and tried to defend himself with the other hand. I'd already kneed him once, but this time I missed, and the blow to his stomach didn't have much effect.

I found myself held by the waist, in the grip of two paws I thought were going to break my spine. I got a whiff of bad breath; he was trying to nibble at me with his disgusting mouth. I turned my head aside and stopped pushing him away so I could grab him around the neck, real tight, and with all the strength I could muster, I bit him on the ear.

His plier-like arms let up as he tried to bring one of them up to his bleeding ear, but I was still hanging on to his neck and now I was the one who had him by the waist, with my legs.

The whole house must have heard him howling, but I could only hear the voices of the men in the garden, who were loudly wondering what the hell was going on.

Martí, yelling and cursing, was trying to get rid of me, hitting me in the back with crazed and merciless fists. He had a bull neck, and he was keeping his muscles tense to keep me from choking him.

The blows to my back forced me to stop, and I let up. Then he shoved me away from him, and I fell on my back, my head grazing the bed. But when he headed for me, blinded with rage, I rolled myself up in a ball and he fell on his face right on the metal bed frame; he was half dazed by the blow.

I jumped up and looked instinctively for something to defend myself with. A cut glass ashtray with sharp corners on the dresser put him out cold as a rock. Blood was spurting out of his head, but the ashtray was unscathed.

I turned him over, face up, and checked out his lapel to see what security agency he was from. Then I took the key out of his pocket and rushed towards the door. Just as I opened it I heard steps and voices from inside the house.

I ran to the window. The two men who had dismantled my car were running towards the front of the house. Between the two floors there were eaves that would break my jump. Even if it had been a smooth wall, I didn't have any other way out.

I let myself down quickly and jumped on the projection trying to flex my legs so I could get all the way to the ground. I landed on the grass without any bones broken, but the robe was all torn up. A creeping rose bush had cushioned me so now those vegetal thorns were added to the porcupine quills.

I started to run, pursued by the screams coming from the room. I went around the house, trying to hide and at the same time to find some opening in the green wall that surrounded the place. But everything was as enclosed as if it were a convent of cloistered nuns. By the time I had decided to jump the wall, the screams and running had left the house and were overtaking the grounds.

Then I twisted my ankle and broke my shoe.

Before me, there was only the night and the hulk of the factory, illuminated with sinister lights. Behind me, the voices had multiplied and the din made me imagine that thousands of eyes were trying to figure out which way I had gone, where I was hiding.

Then I heard the dogs. I headed for the factory. At this point, my ankle didn't hurt, or my head, or the scratches. Just my soul, which is the worst pain a person can experience.

I stopped short. The factory guard was coming towards me

with a mutt on a chain and a lantern that gave off less light than a candle in purgatory. As a matter of fact, it was only good for giving away his presence. I crouched down behind a bush growing among piles of garbage—from behind, things always look like negatives of themselves.

The guard went right by me, with his dog yelping but not sniffing. He followed the path to the rear entrance of the house—the escape I was looking for but couldn't find, shit!

As soon as he went inside, I started to run towards the factory and disappeared through the first opening I could find. Through a low window I got myself into a dark, silent storeroom. A strong and familiar odor put my memory to work, reminding me of going to buy sawdust at the lumbermill for the stove, or passing an open woodshop in summer, or playing in the woodpiles behind warm and shady stores.

Crouched between two huge piles that reached the roof, I broke out in a sweat. In the silence my eyes started to get used to the darkness. Then I heard the muffled noises of the place and the barking of dogs. Then cars starting up and taking off suddenly.

I had already made some visual palpations of a section of the storehouse when I heard the unmistakable saunter of the guard and the dog's tiresome yelping. But man and beast passed by me, as if the brouhaha of the house hadn't affected them in the slightest.

A little later I dared to come out of my hiding place so I could case the joint. I looked out the window I had climbed through and saw that the house was all lit up. Through another window, I could see that the bulk of the factory and the other storerooms were in the dark, resting peacefully, which meant that they were looking for me elsewhere.

Inside, there were stacks of wood everywhere. In the middle, forming two big rows in the center, there were immense packing boxes, all stamped with Malabo Inc., as if they were ready to be loaded or had just been unloaded. Right in front of the metal door, there was a jalopy of a truck.

Dawn was breaking. But I had to wait until the factory was in full swing so I wouldn't be noticed.

I had plenty of time to snoop around. Beside the door there

was a rack with three coveralls and three hats, all khaki color. The private office of the factory was enclosed in a glass booth. Files, shelves, records; freight slips and invoices. Wood imported from the Philippines. Were the Philippines a wood exporting place? Exportation of furniture to Africa, Asia, America with instructions for assembling prefabricated furniture. Wood of every kind: pine, oak, and other types I'd never heard of. Measures, weights, sizes, names of businesses from all over the world. Exotic names of ships. Whole shiploads, roundtrip, with only a few days of difference between arrival and departure.

As the morning advanced, I took notes of figures, measures and sizes, weights and names of ships and businesses. When I put the papers back where they were, an envelope caught my attention; it was full of photocopies of instructions for using tools that didn't have anything to do with wood. I kept one sheet and put the others back inside the envelope. It was dusty and yellowed, as if forgotten among other papers on the shelf, but the words Gòmara Wood were still visible, written in pencil.

I still had time to open one of the boxes. Wood, unpolished. Rough to the touch. Quite different from the planks that made up the piles throughout the factory. It seemed strange that it would be worth it to import that wood from so far away. It must be pretty cheap; so cheap it would splinter. I scratched a piece and with a fingernail I carved a sliver out.

Then the siren went off, and you could hear noises inside the factory. The time had come.

I climbed up some planking so I could look out a high window and see the entrance to the factory. Hydraulic carts loaded with wood were coming out of some of the storerooms. The buzz was getting louder. People dressed in khaki coveralls were swarming down the neat aisles among the sections.

I put on a coverall and hid my hair under one of the caps. I grabbed a handful of invoices and put them on the seat of the truck. I hot-wired it, and with the motor on I opened the gate and took off.

My heart was in my throat, but no one noticed me. I followed the road that I had traced from the window—no problem.

The barriers at the entrance opened automatically without me having to show any papers to the guard at the sentry box, who was wearing a uniform from the same security company.

I waved to the guard with the hand I had the splinter in, and he returned a friendly gesture. Through the rear-view mirror, I could see the barriers slowly going down. No one had raised an alarm.

The same car that was there yesterday was on the side street, but neither of the two men standing alongside it was the Catalan. I passed by calmly. The sun was beginning to warm things up.

IX

Friday morning

"Lònia, what happened to you? You could have told me you weren't coming home last night. Jerònia's back, she's here, at your house."

Our worlds were so different, hers and mine, and I'd lived alone so long that I'd forgotten what it was like to live with someone else. Letting them know what you were doing, calling so they wouldn't worry... And what the hell did I care about Jerònia at this point? What the devil was she doing at my place?

"Listen, Sebastiana..."

"And Quim called from the office. He hassled me when I told him I didn't know where you were."

"Listen..."

"Are you okay? Anything new? Jerònia says she has to talk to you right away, and Quim said..."

"Will you listen, for Christ's sake!" She listened. "Call Quim... no, if he's at the office I'll call him. Don't budge from the house, because if he's not there you'll have to do me a favor. Understand?"

"Yes, sure I understand. But when will you be back? Wait, Jerònia wants to talk to you."

"Not right now."

"Then what shall I tell her? She says my parents..."

"Your parents can fuck off, and Jerònia can mind her own damn business."

I hung up and dialed again. Quim really had a guardian angel's sixth sense. He always turned up when I needed him. If he'd been in the phone booth with me at that moment instead of on

75

the other end of the line, I'd have hugged him. I was trembling with gratitude.

Half an hour later he showed up at the bar I told him about in Esplugues, and half an hour after that, instead of stopping at my place to change, we went to the office.

"Can't you tell me why we're in such a hurry?" I asked.

My gratitude faded when he refused to take me home. I'd left the truck, with the coverall and cap inside, on a street in Esplugues. But when I went into the office I realized it had been futile to try to throw them off the track.

My little lair had never been what you would call high-rent. No carpeting, no indirect lighting, no indoor garden, no air conditioning. But now it was really a wreck, worse than if a cyclone had come through.

The files, that I took such pains to keep in order, had been pulled out and thrown all over the red tile floor. My desk drawers had been forced open and emptied. The chairs were upside-down, for no apparent reason, unless the visiting vandals thought I kept my secrets hidden under the seats. The Miró poster was on the floor, aslant, with the glass shattered and the frame smashed. They'd played football with the books on my shelves. The blank paper and envelopes on the little side table were unusable; someone had had a good time smearing them, one by one, with the lipsticks I kept in the bathroom. And when they ran.out of clean paper, they'd turned to decorating my freshly painted walls with red scribbles. To finish the job, they'd even stuffed pages torn out of the telephone book into the toilet.

Quim was waiting for my explosion, but I only had energy to swear in a low voice and cry with rage.

"They weren't looking for anything in particular," he finally said. "They just wanted to scare you."

But that wasn't true. Quim still didn't know half the story, because I hadn't wanted to talk in the taxi. They wanted to scare me, all right, but they were also looking for something.

I dried my eyes so I could see better, and started to look for my dossier on Antal. The file was under a pile of papers, empty.

Then the two of us started to look hastily for the antique dealer's papers. We needed more than God's help to plow through that bedlam of papers, but nothing was missing.

"The pictures," I said with my voice on a thread. "Let's see which ones are missing."

When we'd gathered and gone through all of them, only the ones of Gòmara at Antal's funeral were missing.

"And now you're going to explain it all to me, right?" Quim said to me.

But I couldn't speak. I felt completely dominated by an overwhelming sensation of fear that left my throat totally tight.

"These people, Quim... I don't want to stay here another second... They could come back... Let's go to my place... They don't have the address and the telephone isn't in my name... "

"How'd they get the address of the office?"

"They even got my license."

Quim's astonished eyes would have made me laugh if I hadn't been holding back the sobs.

"What in the hell did you get yourself into?"

It was then that a fleeting shadow of joy passed through my sore, aching body. I'd gotten myself into a bramble bush, but I was about to discover something really big, important. I rifled through my pants pockets; the papers I'd stuffed in them felt good to my hands. I took out the piece of wood and put it in an envelope. Then I remembered the splinter. It could get infected.

"See if there are any tweezers in the bathroom," I said to Quim. "And alcohol, or mercurochrome... "

It was deep in my fingertip, and it was pretty big. I hoped it hadn't all been for nothing.

The drop of blood that came out after I got the splinter out reminded me of Martí, and the fear returned. The professional joy of a few minutes ago had vanished, and all I had left was depression over the state of the devastated office.

I grabbed the antique dealer's dossier and headed for the door. Quim was standing in the middle of the room like a statue.

"Are you coming or not?" I said to him.

"Can't you even tell me where you left the car?" he asked me while we waited for a taxi.

"They've got that too."

"Fuck!"

While I was showering—Christ, was my ankle sore, and the soap really made all those scratches sting!—Quim prepared Sebastiana and Jerònia so well that when I came out of the bathroom, breakfast was ready and the two were respectfully silent.

Between munching on bread and jelly and sipping tea with honey, I gave them the gory details about everything that had happened since Quim had disappeared.

"Why didn't you take his gun, too?" he interrupted when I got to the part about being held at Gòmara's and hitting Martí with an ash tray.

"Me? A gun? Not on your life."

"Oh, Lònia, Lònia," he sighed, as if he were saying *you lunatic.*

When I showed him the papers, and especially the photocopied instructions, he concluded:

"It's obvious that you have to let this case go. Leave the antique dealer be, Lònia. And we'll have to move, whatever, but let it go. It's too dangerous."

"What are you talking about? Now's when I want to keep going. That son of a bitch—and I don't have anything against bitches—I'm going to get that Gòmara, Quim, I swear it. And I won't get a good night's sleep until I twist Martí's balls... "

"Lònia, Lònia... " Quim repeated.

"It's personal now, and besides I'm curious. I want to know what's going on between Gòmara and Gaudí, and I'd like to get my car back. So don't try to persuade me otherwise."

He didn't look too convinced. But now that I'd had a shower and something to eat, things looked a lot better. He was right, we'd have to move.

"I'll take care of everything," he stuttered, and when I didn't object, he looked happier.

Meantime, I'd investigate the REC company, an import-export agency, and I'd have to get into the international docks. And I needed another car, damn them! And I'd need to tell the Detective League as well as the cops I'd lost my license...

But by now Jerònia was running out of patience. After all, she'd come here all the way from Majorca...

"Sebastiana's parents... I couldn't convince them to wait any longer, and to keep them from turning the case over to the police, I had to tell them you'd found her."

"And I told them I'd go back to Majorca with her!" Sebastiana burst into tears.

It didn't do any good to try to help people. To hope things would change, that there would be more justice and everything would be simpler was a dream, as eternal as it was useless.

I was about at the point of sending them all to hell, including the restless parents. But Sebastiana's helpless and overwhelmed look made me put up one last resistance. It was a dramatic situation which could, with a little good will on the part of the old-timers and Jerònia, turn out more or less okay. But the old-timers and Jerònia didn't dare break the rules established centuries ago that held them to a tight-assed morality that handed down to them all their decisions ready-made, sealed in plexiglass. Incredible as it was, it was easier for them to follow their ancestral customs, no matter how complicated, than to look for a smoother way. They were suffering, and they were making everybody in their power suffer too.

"Did you tell them that their daughter is pregnant because she was raped?"

"No, I didn't dare. They would be horrified. Besides they wouldn't believe it . . . "

"They'll have to believe it, unless she has an abortion."

"No, they'll believe she's pregnant, all right, but not that she was raped."

"I see. They're the kind that believe if a woman is raped, it's because she went along with it."

I believed that once myself. Until one day I said it in front of Mercè, and she tore my opinion into shreds. She kneaded my arguments like Uncle Pere used to knead bread, with lots of strength. But Mercè's strength was moral, and she left my soul in pieces all over the floor.

"That's what they think." Sebastiana's voice was as pale and deathlike as her face. "My father has always said that. But I, I, maybe I did give in too soon, but I was afraid he'd hurt me . . . He was beating me up, and he threatened me with a knife . . . ." Sobs kept her from going on and shame turned her face crimson.

I would like to have told her how I had freed myself from

Martí yesterday, and how afraid I'd been when I fell down totally defenseless, at the foot of that bed.

Instead, I asked her,

"Have you ever heard of Maria Goretti?"

She shook her head no, and Jerònia explained with great love and pride the epic of the young girl who allowed herself to be killed rather than raped. Sebastiana hung her head.

"When the nuns told me that story," I interrupted, "I remember that I made the comment that that girl became a saint and martyr because she was crazy. They kicked me out of school and my mother was horrified to have such a sacrilegious daughter. But I still think the same thing. You're not to blame for having consented, Sebastiana. The guy who forced you is to blame. Get that into your head and hold that head high. And don't let your parents or anyone else"—and I looked at Jerònia—"tell you otherwise."

She seemed like she'd been relieved of a heavy load, but she was still so unsure of the world she was in.

"What should I do, then?" she asked hopefully.

"Come back to Majorca with me," Jerònia cut in, full of resolve. "It's the only solution."

"It's the only solution you have to offer. But she can find others that would be better for her."

I suddenly felt a lot like arguing.

"Like what?" Jerònia had gotten the same urge and she was making me take sides in a question I was already too quagmired in.

"Stay in Barcelona and have an abortion. In her case there aren't any legal problems. And she can start to live on her own," I said without beating around the bush.

"That solution goes against her morals," Jerònia said.

"To hell with it, then. I have troubles of my own. I've done my job by finding her."

The morning was dwindling away, and I had lots to do. Obligations before devotions, ran the popular, shrewd and realistic wisdom. Just the opposite of the kind of stuff the priests were still preaching before the throne amidst the flapping of angels' wings, and that people like Jerònia repeated like an echo.

Finally, Sebastiana decided to stay in Barcelona.

"Can I stay here with you?" What could I say? But she wouldn't get an abortion.

Jerònia went back to Majorca, leaving an open plane ticket in case Sebastiana changed her mind. I was left unsatisfied and very worried about the responsibility I hadn't known how to get rid of, and I made some phone calls and went to see Pepa.

The Wharf of Wood, converted into a palm-lined avenue, reminded me of my early days in Barcelona, when my roommates used to recite the poem, "You all haven't kept wood at the wharf."*

The palm trees, still scrawny, made me homesick for the luxurious, ancient walkway of the Sagrera and the plaza in front of the Exchange in Palma. Palm trees need lots of time and patience to acquire body and character. Like people.

I went up to the office on Colom Avenue, and while I was waiting I could see the masts all jammed together at the Club Nàutic.

I had only been there once, to see Quico's and Jerònia's boat (another Jerònia! and as different as night and day in spite of the names). Their bridal registry was at a store that sold nautical items, and they had been honeymooning on board the double-masted Puma Eixerit for about five years now, sailing all over the world.

This Jerònia had been my roommate, and she was studying journalism with such admirable dedication that I signed up too. But I'd gotten tired of it by the second semester. I don't like to learn how to do things, I like to do them, and sometimes I pay the price.

Just about a year ago, I'd been about ready to toss in with them and their adventures and go meet them in Peru so we could visit the Galapagos Islands together. I was really more attracted by the change of atmosphere than the exotic islands.

It had been four years by then since I'd gotten my license, excited about all the adventures I would have. But four years later

---

* Lines from an extremely well-known poem by Joan Salvat-Papasseit, suggested by the name of the wharf.

the adventures had turned into bureaucracy, just like in Mr. Marí's office in Palma. I had a nice little business that was making it, but the job was as monotonous and boring as working in a bank or on an assembly line. I was disillusioned and fed up with it.

The very same thing had happened to me with my dreams about flying on planes, with a blue uniform and little round cap. Three months at the Son Sant Joan airport, hanging around with all those crazies, had been more than enough to rid me of those illusions.

Yet in the end I hadn't taken on the adventure of the Galapagos. I didn't dare give everything up. I was afraid that if that was disappointing too, I wouldn't have anywhere to go, or any roots to tie me down.

To console myself for my unconfessed cowardice, I decided that everyone has their own adventures inside, and you don't need to go looking for them. I'd stick with my job.

Seen from a distance, the moored and anchored boats seemed immobile, indifferently taking in the sun. I knew there was always a rocking motion on the water even in Barcelona's closed in, oily port. I wished I were in Australia, where Quico and Jerònia were now, doing radio programs in Catalan, for Christ's sake! so they could pay for repairs to the Eixerit, which was all worn out. I wanted to forget about the other Jerònia, Sebastiana's rotten melodrama, the gangsters who had wrecked my office, the antique dealer who was still telling me lies—she was lying, all right, or at least she wasn't telling me the whole story.

"Miss Guiu . . . "

The voice brought me back to the freight office. When I turned around, I was blinded by the sun's reflection on the smooth surface of the water.

When I went into her office, Maria Josep, Pepa for short, recognized me. She couldn't remember my name, but she knew my face.

We spoke for a few minutes about the only period when we'd been in contact, the only time I'd gotten involved in politics. I was working with an international solidarity group, and Pepa worked in their office.

We'd gotten along well. We'd gone out to dinner together a few times and shared our secrets. Then I got tired of it, or I got scared, and stopped going to the meetings. We hadn't seen each other since then, about seven years ago. But I could tell by her smile that the warmth was still there.

"Really? You're a detective? How exciting!"

"Huh!" I replied sincerely.

And I started the professional consultations.

The weight coincided with the cubic contents and the cubic contents with the bulk. But only for certain kinds of wood.

"How can I find out the routes and the cargo of these ships on these dates?"

"Look it up in *El Vigía.*"

"What's that?"

"It's a daily paper here at the port," she smiled. "I have them all."

I closed myself up in a storeroom where the periodicals were kept until the office closed up. It was like an oven, but I discovered a whole new world. Sometime when I have time, when I'm not looking for specific information, I'd like to have a closer look at all this. . . .

I left the room sweaty and covered with dust. Before I left, I asked Pepa to do me one last favor.

"Could you get me a pass to go into the international docks? The commercial ones, I mean . . . "

"It won't be easy, but I'll try."

"Thanks. If it all turns out okay, I'll tell you the whole story. For the moment, though, it has to be kept secret."

"Okay. Don't worry on my account. Call me tomorrow."

X

Friday noon

"Quim called. Call him at this number."

In one morning Sebastiana had miraculously recovered from the depression brought on by Jerònia's presence. Now she was in good spirits and keeping busy. She had cleaned and straightened up the whole house—but listen, tomorrow the cleaning lady's coming!

"I have to do something with my time."

"Take a walk, or read, shit!"

"I did go out," and she led me to the kitchen.

The table was set with a great Majorcan salad in the middle and half a dozen stuffed eggplants au gratin on each plate.

"There's no meat," she reassured me. "And I bought it with my own stash."

"I'm sure, since there's not a cent in the house."

I was exhausted, but the sight of those succulent goodies revived me. First, though, I called Quim. The number wasn't familiar to me.

"Where are you?"

"At your new office. Right on the corner of Aragó and Passeig de Gràcia!"

"Are you crazy? That must cost a fortune!"

"Not much at all, if you only pay half."

"Listen, I still want to be the boss, and this is a real bad deal, Quim."

"As long as you're the one with the license, you'll be the boss. Come on, don't be so reactionary, let me stop being a lackey . . .

an exploited one at that... Listen, I'm just finishing moving all the stuff, but there were two calls at the office. One from the antique dealer. The other..."

"The other one?" Why had my heart dropped to my shoes?

"The other one from the cops. They wanted to come and see you but I told them you wouldn't be there until four."

"Four? Oh, Quim, it's already three thirty and I haven't had lunch."

"Me neither."

"I'm so sleepy!"

"Hey, I'm sorry. I'm going there now, so at least someone will be there. But I don't mind telling you it would be a good idea for you to show up too."

"What the hell do they want?"

"I wouldn't be surprised if Gòmara put them up to it. He's a big shot."

"A tacky big shot."

With great pain and much to Sebastiana's chagrin, I abandoned Majorcan salad, eggplant and bed. The clanking of the bus helped me forget about the aborted meal and nap and I started getting some answers ready for the cops.

The office had been my headquarters for five years, and now it was as empty as my stomach. I felt a sadness that made my eyes water.

"Don't tell me you're sorry to leave this dump?" Quim was genuinely surprised.

"I'm always sorry about things ending," I said for myself. "But I don't like things that last forever either."

Quim looked a little mocking as well as surprised at so much transcendentalism. After all, it had been an eternal five years of inertia, begun with great illusions but full of boring hours and boring jobs, requiring no skill. Five rotten miserable years between those walls now all smudged with lipstick.

"Did you get my stuff from the bathroom?"

Putting your feet on the ground, touching everyday things, sometimes was good for getting rid of what I once would have called vital anguish. Now I would call it cosmic bullshit.

"A bag from the Corte Inglés* full of lipsticks! Jesus, what a mania, Lònia!"

I looked at the street. The Ronda was full of people and cars. That was a good spot in spite of everything, and very cheap considering the location. When I started doing investigations, I usually headed down towards the Port from Plaza Catalunya, but in the last three years, I'd been going up into the Eixample neighborhood and to the beltway communities. Now, I had a mixture of everything: the city in my hands. Except that I had to hide.

Things were on sale everywhere, and people were all carrying plastic bags like the one I had lipstick in. There was a mania for buying, for spending the money that hadn't been quite enough for a vacation. At least a person had the consolation of possessing something, and of believing it had been a bargain. I felt that way about the Gòmara affair.

Looking at those absurdly restless people, contented with a few mirages and such cheap dreams, made me feel that I was looking into a mirror. I was just like anyone else in that river of self-satisfied people.

But I didn't have time to sink into that troubling feeling. The doorbell resounded in the emptiness of the room, and Quim hurried to answer it.

The two characters looked more like delinquents than real officers. But they showed me a license and I had to put up with the one with his face covered with pimples, the other with bony eyebrows, and the body odor of the two of them.

"Movin'?" the one with the eyebrows asked, sounding illiterate.

"We're doing a general housecleaning," Quim said before I had a chance to give any unnecessary explanations.

That meant he didn't like that visit a bit, either.

Why had they come in person instead of citing me to the inspector of the commission, as usual?

"What's up?" I was glad I didn't have any chairs to offer them.

"Miss Lònia Guiu?"

"Yes."

"Do you have a detective's license?"

* A major chain of department stores

"Of course. But that's a useless question. Surely you looked it up in your files before you came, and you know very well that I have a license."

"May I see it?"

"I always keep it in my safe deposit box at the bank. I wouldn't like to lose it."

"Then be careful who you mess with, or you might lose it for good."

The pimply one had a whiny voice which didn't go at all with his ruddy face, shiny with sweat. But he spoke better than the other one, as if he had learned a few phrases by heart.

"Is that what you came to tell me?"

"We've come because a complaint has been filed against you. For trespassing and serious injuries."

I thought of Martí and I could see that angular glass ash tray against the dusty red floor of my office. It was a relief to know he hadn't died, even though that's just what he deserved.

"I thought complaints were made at the commissioner's office. What a privilege to be told personally," Quim said.

"Who are you?" said the one with the eyebrows.

He shoved his hands into the pockets of his gray synthetic bush jacket, full of the kind of stains that won't come out. He was playing a tough guy.

"I'm her partner."

"It's not on file that this is a partnership," said Pimples, recovering his sing-songy voice.

"So you did look things up before you came," I said mockingly. "He's my secretary, not my partner."

"So she's the one who wears the pants around here," Eyebrows said to Quim. "There are all kinds of men," he raised those eyebrows as far as they would go and scorn made his eyes get smaller.

"Exactly. Some are more human than others." Quim replied, winking at me.

A silence followed that made me even madder. It was as if they were trying to try my patience. Strangely, I had plenty of patience all of a sudden, and the fear had dissipated. I could even see the fun in the situation. I was positive there hadn't been any complaint. Gòmara just wanted me out of circulation and he didn't know how to do it. All to the good.

"Okay," I finally said. "What are we supposed to do about the complaint?"

"You admit it?"

"What?"

"That you entered a house without permission and attacked one of the inhabitants?"

I was speaking to Pimples while Eyebrows snooped around the paintings on the walls.

"What house?" I asked. "What inhabitants? If you don't give me more details, I don't know what you're talking about. The place, the time, specific actions. And the people. Those are my rights."

Pimples clucked his tongue, pissed off. The other one came up to me and with his clumsy language said something like this:

"Listen here kid. If you ain't careful we'll take your license away. You can't just go 'round hasslin' people. If you were my chick, I can tell you . . . "

"But I'm not," I broke out laughing.

"What do you want with Mr. Gòmara?" he said furiously, humiliated by my laughter.

Pimples gave him a dirty look.

"Now we're getting somewhere! So it's Ernest Gòmara who made a complaint? Okay, I'll tell you why I'm investigating him, maybe he'll leave me alone. A client of mine suspects he's making it with his wife."

The two officers stared at each other, unable to hide their surprise. Their look made me add, without even thinking,

"Or with his son . . . ".

The surprise changed to total astonishment, especially for the one with the eyebrows.

"With a man? Mr. Gòmara? Impossible!" he exclaimed.

Quim, hanging on to the bathroom door, couldn't keep from laughing.

"Why not? Didn't you just say there are all kinds of men?"

I noticed the air was getting thick, and the pimply one had no sense of humor.

"You think you can pull our leg, Miss. But you don't mess with the law, and you should know that better than anyone. The only way to annul the complaint—or get around it"—he twisted his collar as a sign of complicity—"is for you to tell us why you're following him. And the reason has to be realistic, of course."

"I already told you: a client of mine who suspects some sleeping around. And don't ask me who the client is, because as you must know better than anyone, I can't be obliged to reveal a professional secret."

"Okay, it's up to you. Now if you take my advice, you'll drop this investigation. It's nasty to wash other people's dirty clothes... Don't say I didn't warn you."

He wiped the sweat off his brow.

As we heard their steps going downstairs, Quim commented:

"When Gòmara finds you've moved and those two guys didn't even take the initiative of finding out where, he'll have apoplexy."

I looked out that window onto the Ronda for the last time. The bustling people made me envious; they looked happy.

I returned the antique dealer's call from the new office.

"I was wondering if you'd found out anything new," she said amiably.

"I'm on the trail. I lost the car we were following because of you, and now it turns out the owner isn't the man you're looking for. You'll have to wait a while. Oh, and don't call me at the office any more. I won't be there."

"Where can I call you, then?"

"I'll be in touch with you."

"But listen... "

I didn't listen.

I looked at the new office. It was clean and bright. At the rate he was going, Quim would have everything in order by tomorrow. But I was so tired I couldn't even praise him for it.

"Don't you like it?"

"Yes, I like it a lot. Thanks, thanks a million. You're a good kid." I was so tired my eyes were misting.

"You don't have to cry. That's what friends are for, right? Now, you go on home and don't think about those creeps any more. At least until tomorrow."

I left, but I didn't go home. The Majorcan salad, the egg-plants, my bed... not yet.

At the lab, Joan was surprised when I gave him the sliver. "Are you in a rush? We're closed tomorrow."

"How about today? Couldn't you look at it for me today?"

"You always come here in a big rush, Lònia. If the boss knew I put you ahead of everybody else... "

That meant yes.

"What time will you bring them?" I asked.

After eight, closing time. It was six now. It wasn't worth going home for two hours. I called Sebastiana.

"Don't worry, it'll be good for dinner," I had to console her.

She told me she was tired of being all alone. Could she come wherever I was?"

Again, she was in a quagmire about what to do, how to deal with her situation. She boggled my mind as we sat in a bar for two hours on Rambla Catalunya. She was a jumble of fears, in-securities and vacillations.

I cursed my bones for having been such a softy with her, for having been unable to just leave her to her own devices, for not having sided with Jerònia that she should go back to Majorca to receive her punishment and her forgiveness for something that wasn't her fault, but that's the way it is, kid, that's life.

With my whole body aching, I was hearing without really listening to Sebastiana's steady stream of broken words. My thoughts strayed to the Baroness of Prenafeta, who maybe was the key to everything. But to what? I thought. And to the third man, whom I hadn't found yet, but whom the antique dealer would surely want me to find.

Now I see I should have an abortion, because at least all alone I can make it, but with a baby, why did it occur to me to tell Gòmara's cops that he was getting it on with a son? But I can't get it out of my head that it's murder, and I'll always feel guilty, I already do, and by the way what was Arquer doing at the funeral, it wasn't an accident, what clinic did they take him to? I'd have to go back to see the Baroness again. And I'd have to find the third man, Neus would have work again, but how could I send her to take pictures of the people around Gòmara, guarded and walled up like he was surrounded by armed guards, even cops, I'd have to go see my policeman friend, too, no, I doubt if my father would send the police after me, that's what I need... problems with the police because of this nitwit, as if I didn't have enough problems of my own, I could just drop by to ask him if anyone has made a complaint against me, etc., etc., and my muscles relaxed, rocked like the boats at the docks, not by the oily, iridescent water but by the monotony in Sebastiana's voice, which was now saying you look tired, and here I am yakking but I'm so confused and I don't have anybody but you to help me, and I'm so alone maybe it would be better if I died, because even if they found the guy who raped me, I wouldn't want to marry him. I couldn't love him, and marriage is for your whole life...

My body's exhaustion shut off my thinking compartment. But the clock striking startled me. It was eight.

"It's eucalyptus," Joan said, joining us in the bar. "Have you become an ecologist now?"

He wanted to take me out to dinner. We ended up all three going to my place to share the Majorcan salad and the eggplants. I fell asleep half way through the meal.

PART TWO

XI

Saturday

The first thing I did when I arrived in Barcelona from Majorca was to go to Benson & Juds and ask for a job. It was the company we had worked for as correspondents in Barcelona and for that reason I didn't trust them too much. But by the same token I figured they wouldn't be too particular about who they hired. Besides, my experience with the Marí Agency would be useful as a recommendation.

They had more people than they needed at Benson, but they were nice; since I was recommended by a cooperating agency, they wrote me a letter of introduction to another company, not exactly an information agency, they said, but more or less related. No sooner said than done; by the time I'd unpacked my bags at the students' apartment, I had a job. My new companions marvelled at my luck, and congratulated me. But after a few days, when they found out what kind of a job it was, they almost threw me out.

How could I have accepted that? At first I tried to defend myself: it was an honorable, worthy job, just like any other. Honorable? Worthy? It was defending the interests of the real thieves against the people's right to possess things, just like everyone else. The petty theft I was supposed to discover and turn in to the big department stores, they called recoveries. And they had friends at the university who put themselves through school by reselling recovered clothes. Us, too: look at this sweater. If the regular price is double what they sell it for during their sales and they still make money, it means they're selling it for more than a hundred percent over cost; isn't that robbery? Why shouldn't I wear the same kind of clothes my classmates who had rich parents wear? Rich from robbing, of course.

I thought the argument was pretty flighty, and I said so. The verbal discussion almost became physical when they found out the security agency was run by off-duty policemen. Collaborator! You're a rotten collaborator and it's dangerous to have you here in the apartment, the cops could come by any day to have coffee with you after we've covered the university's patio with pamphlets.

I didn't understand what they were talking about. Don't you know what the police do at the university, damn you? And at the police stations? Keep order and protect people? Sure! Depends on what order and what people! My roommates' yelling could be heard all the way over at Saint Anthony's Market, and I was scared.

They didn't go so far as to throw me out, but when I was there they didn't speak to me or each other. And above all, don't tell your friends where you live or who you live with, understand? they ordered. Don't spy on us. And they locked up all their papers instead of leaving them around on tables and chairs, like before.

The women who watched the customers, especially other women, in the big department stores, dressed like customers and pretended to shop and rummage through merchandise. Most were daughters or relatives of policemen. If we saw someone take something without paying for it, we were supposed to stop them, without creating a scene, and take them to some offices downstairs where there were two policemen, who were paid a supplement. The truth is that I was always a little uneasy about leaving the shoplifter in the hands of the cops, even though they assured me they didn't do anything to them, they didn't even arrest them. It was just a way to teach them a lesson and at the most they would let the family know for the record and embarrass them.

One day my roommates took me to the university. There were lots of people in the patio arguing, and all of a sudden a bunch of papers rained down from the upper, shuttered corridors. Some people were putting posters of brown wrapping paper on the columns and everybody started clapping. Then, amidst the applause, you could hear a whistle and everybody scattered, as if the falling pamphlets were a silent hailstorm. My friends had disappeared, and there I was leaning against a column stiff as a board looking around me, astonished. Suddenly, four giants dressed in gray came into the patio with their faces covered and swinging their clubs. The patio was deserted, the plants in the gardens covered with papers. The four gray figures, like monolithic solid blocks of granite, were coming toward me. I must have run, terrified, toward an interior hallway, because I heard screams, insults, blows, running, as I hid who knows how under a table in an empty classroom.

That evening, Margalida showed me the bruise on her shoulder from the club. The next day, in the store, I caught two girls who had taken some plastic earrings. After I'd taken them to the two cops on duty, instead of going back to work, I hung around where they were. The cops didn't touch them, but first one of them put the handcuffs ceremoniously on the table. They threatened to lock them up, and they bawled them out for how ashamed their parents would be, and one after the other they put all their virtues in doubt, and then their mothers'.

I left the section when the two kids coughed up the price—truly exorbitant—of the plastic earrings, in tears. The next day I didn't go back to work.

But while the job had lasted, I'd made friends with one policeman I'd worked with two or three times. He was a guy about my age, as inexperienced and idiotic as I was. I didn't see him again until three years later, when I tried to intercede on behalf of Margalida, who had been arrested and accused of subversion. He had done well for himself; now he only had to do one job to make it till the end of the month. He couldn't help me then, or didn't want to. But when I decided to get myself established, he did everything he could to help me get a license. In the five years I'd been practicing, I'd seen him or spoken with him on the phone maybe three or four times, always in dire straits. The bad feelings I had for people in that profession as a result of Margalida's back injury had developed into a rational aversion. Even though I still liked that guy, I couldn't forget what he did for a living.

I'd dreamt about him all night, because I knew sooner or later

97

I'd have to pay him a visit, first about the complaint and then about the lost license. The Majorcan salad, the stuffed eggplants and exhaustion did the rest.

I got up though I didn't feel like it. While I drank my coffee I decided to leave the visit for another day, and I felt better.

Sebastiana came up to me while I was looking through telephone books. She looked sleepy, but before she had a chance to say good morning, she rushed to the bathroom and I could hear the characteristic sounds of someone trying to throw up. Poor kid, it was starting already.

She came back in after a while, with her face washed but still looking helpless.

"How long have you been vomiting?"

"This is the first time. It must be the Majorcan salad from last night."

Holy innocence.

"Listen . . . that friend of yours, Joan . . . "

"Yeah? I'm sorry, Sebastiana, I was so tired yesterday. Was he mad?"

"No, not at all, but when we'd put you to bed, he told me he'd like to sleep with me."

Men had no self-control at all. If they didn't make it with one, they tried the next.

"What did you say?"

"No, of course! He said I was silly, and that you didn't have to play it so straight. What does that mean?"

"It's what people like Joan say when they can't take no for an answer. Come on, eat a little, you'll feel better."

"Even thinking of eating makes me sick."

"Then call Mercè. She'll tell you what to do." I didn't feel a bit like playing nurse.

I kept on looking in the phone book. I found it under Rec Security, Urgell Street. I looked on the map to see what block of Urgell that number would be. It was between Sepúlveda and Gran Via. Since the number was odd, it would be on the left, going up. On the Llobregat side; that is Urgell-Gran Via, Sea-Llobregat.

I called Pepa before leaving the house.

"I'm sorry, but there's no pass," she told me. "But maybe if you pretend you're lost you can get in . . . or by sea . . . There are some sailors who take tourists on little cruises around the port."

"In the little boats they call golondrines?"

"No, the ones alongside the Columbus replica. Smaller boats. You'll see . . . ."

"Okay, thanks a lot. But can I ask you something else? Does eucalyptus correspond to the weights and measures we looked at the other day?"

There was a moment of silence.

"No, not by a long shot," she finally said. "It's a lot lighter. Twenty or twenty-five percent less weight for the volume you told me. Even less. Want me to figure it out exactly?"

"No, it won't be necessary. Thanks."

"The truth is, I should look more carefully, because it's not a common wood . . . "

"No, not at all, is it?"

The taxi cost me a fortune. That's the price you have to pay when your car is ruined, you don't feel like waiting for a bus—who knows when it'll get around to coming—and your claustrophobia keeps you from taking the metro.

I had to ask the doorman which floor Rec Security was on and he told me they didn't open until late morning.

"It's almost eleven," I said.

"Yeah, they might be here soon. The fact is they don't have regular hours."

Continually wiping the sweat off his brow—just watching him made me sweat too—he told me they must have more work than they needed, there sure was a need for security in the city. I do think people exaggerate it, though. Have you ever been robbed? He hadn't, even though he wasn't especially careful and went out whenever he wanted to. He thought the whole thing was a smokescreen to cover up more important things.

He chatted with me for nearly half an hour, and he even invited me into his little office. I have a fan, we'll be cooler.

But I told him I had another errand to do and I'd come back later. First, though, he wanted to know why I wanted a guard, because depending on what it was for, he would gladly be my guard, a pretty girl like me shouldn't go around alone anyway.

I left the vestibule laughing. I'd gladly have slapped his face, but at the moment I needed someone in the building on my side, just in case.

I ordered tea in the bar across the street. Maybe the warmth of the drink would contrast with the hot air . . . And I don't know whether it was the scalded herbs or the two Filipinos I saw go into the building, but I suddenly got so flushed I almost passed out. One was from Orient Sunshine and the other was a long-legged guy all gussied up, dressed in white from head to toe.

I waited a while longer. I decided I would go in when ten people, either coming or going, had gone through the door.

"They opened a while ago," said the flirtatious doorman, winking at me. "Just after you left."

It looked more like an old bachelors' place than a business office, and the cleaning lady hadn't visited for a while. Pretentious but uncared for; the desire to make it welcoming had been quite forgotten. There wasn't a table to receive clients, or a filing cabinet, or even an office desk.

A kid who didn't look much like a bodyguard greeted me. Small and scrawny, he smelled like he'd broken a bottle of cologne on his head.

"What do you want?" I could tell by his voice he didn't feel much like doing his job.

"I want to talk to the owner."

"He's not here."

"What do you have to do to hire a guard?"

"What do you want one for?"

"Are you the one who writes up the contracts? At least you could have me sit down. I'm a potential customer."

He walked away and disappeared inside, leaving me standing there. Would he come back? With the boss? What if the boss was the Filipino from Orient Sunshine?

But he wasn't. It was the long-legged guy. And here I thought all Filipinos were short and smiley.

"We don't hire guards out one at a time here. And we only protect important, and solvent, businesses," he said greeting me in very good Spanish.

"Who told you I only wanted one, and that I'm not important and solvent?"

"What business is it? And why did they send you to take care of this matter?"

"Are you the owner? Because if you are, you sure have a strange way of getting customers. And if you're not, I don't think the boss is going to be too happy with you."

We played that game a while longer. At one point I was about to drop Gòmara's name, but common sense told me not to. I left without knowing much more than when I went in, except that I had confirmed that it wasn't a normal business at all. In the vestibule, I decided to get my compensation for having been patient with the doorman. For starters, I approached his little office smiling from ear to ear.

"It's even hotter upstairs," I said, fanning myself with my hand.

"Do you want to come in?" he set me on a stool right in front of the fan. "Well, any success?"

"I wouldn't have thought a foreigner could put together a business like that," I said indifferently.

"A foreigner?"

"That Filipino dressed in white."

"He's not the boss! Did he tell you that? He's putting you on!"

"That's what I thought. And he sure isn't looking for any new customers. Who is the boss, then?"

"You're from Majorca, right? That's a beautiful place."

There I was again. As soon as one of those regional words slipped out I got the honeymoon story, the pearls, the caves. And pastries, the *enciamades*.

"Are you from Majorca itself?"

I'd lost count of how many times I'd had to explain that if I was Majorcan I had to be from Majorca itself. The island is one thing and the city of Majorca is another.

"They make *enciamades* in that bakery over there like the ones from Majorca."

"They don't make *enciamades* in Majorca."

"Come on, now, you're joking."

After I'd explained to him that what they make in Majorca are *ensaïmades*, and they're called that because they're made with *saïm*, which is how we say lard, I blocked that theme and brought him around to what I wanted to talk about.

"Who did you say is the owner of Rec Security?"

"Was. Because the poor guy . . . he didn't come here much, because he had lots of other businesses. This was like a hobby for him, a game . . . "

"Is he dead?"

"Dead as a doornail, they say. He always gave me a cigar when he came. And this fan, he gave me. He was a big shot, but a nice guy. Poor Mr. Felip!"

"Antal?"

"You knew him? He was a nice guy, wasn't he?"

"Yeah, real nice!"

"So you didn't have to deal with that guy in white, did you? Not at all. Mr. Felip was too nice, he felt sorry for people and gave them jobs without watching out for who they were or what they were like. The business'll go to pot now, you'll see, because those people don't work much, I'm telling you."

"Somebody else'll take over the business, don't worry. His partner Gòmara, maybe . . . "

"Gòmara, Gòmara? Oh, yeah, I know who you mean. But he wasn't a partner, just a customer, that's all."

"You know a lot, don't you?"

"Listen, if you spend all day here, you end up knowing everything, even if you don't want to. And I'm not a busy-body, myself, but . . . . "

In spite of the layer of oil, the motion of the sea and the coolness of the water were pleasant. Neus had brought her grandmother's umbrella, and we looked like three eccentric tourists who were trying to discover some new beauty among the traditional, assumed ugliness of a commercial port.

Unpretentious ships, strangely shaped, barges spotted with rust, cranes, floating trash, and above it all, the screaming gulls.

Seeing the port from the little boat that didn't come up out of the water more than a foot or so was so different from seeing it from a tall ship, big as a city. I was fascinated by that storage stack, by the height of the ship, by the mechanical grandeur of the crane. When this was all ruins, people of the future would be entranced by it just like we were now when we saw pyramids and talaiots.* And I was anticipating them . . .

"We can't go beyond here," said the boatman. Suddenly I remembered I was here to do a job.

I looked with the binoculars towards the international docks. And there it was, moored at the space that said El Vigia. The exact same letters I had seen on the freight invoices in the factory: Medium.

Without saying anything I slipped a bill into the sailor's hand, gesturing him on with my hand.

The boats, laden with fish, used to go swish-swash as they came in at sunset. The sea odor was fresh and healthy then, not smelly like now. But the setting sun worked miracles, changing the shitty air into rosy haze and the layer of oil into iridescent water with silver reflections.

Bilge was being pumped out of the Medium. A haughty crane was swinging an enormous container in the air, labeled Gòmara Wood. Neus took pictures of the sailors while Sebastiana held the umbrella. I was thinking how tough things were going to be if everything was in containers. That's what it looked like, and if so I'd have to go back to Gòmara's factory, which would be a lot harder than a boat trip through the port.

A sailor yelled out at us. Another threw an empty bottle at us, and Neus, the intended target, shook her fist at him. Our boatman turned the boat around immediately, but I had time to see that the cargo was coming from storehouse number two, pushed by tractors with hydraulic antennae.

Sebastiana gave the umbrella back to Neus. She was white as a sheet. She put her hand up to her mouth and leaned over the rail, contributing generously to the filth in the water.

* Prehistoric monoliths found in the Balearic Islands

103

XII

Saturday night

I would have liked Quim to come with me, but I didn't invite him. He not only wouldn't have come, he wouldn't have let me go either. So I put comfortable clothes on and filled up my pockets with the electric poker, the crowbar, the spray and the lantern and went back to the port by way of Can Tunis.

The port water smelled even worse, and the dirty haze, colder now, formed a halo around the dim lampposts.

It's amazing how easy it is to get into places you're not supposed to go into. There wasn't a single guard, sailor, or anyone to keep me company. Just the dark shadow of a stray cat here and there, slinking around among the piles, like me.

But there was plenty going on around the *Medium*. Amid the silence and tranquility of the docks and the sea, the ship was still being loaded.

I went into storehouse number two: it was already empty. I cursed the hardworking sailors and longshoremen, who forced me to go on board. The storehouse doors were closing, and it must have been ages since they'd oiled the hinges. Inside, darkness and the day's heat, captured in there. Outside, the hustle and bustle went on: another squeaky door, the buzz of the tractors and the clanging of chains. But the only window in the storehouse opened to the silent, empty wharf, so I'd have to look for a crack on the side where the noise was coming from; they'd opened the next storeroom and were continuing the loading operation.

The containers had the same logo: Gòmara Wood.

Two hours passed very slowly, stressful for me. Worse for the longshoremen, I suppose, who weren't busting their asses, and I don't blame them. But suddenly the work stopped. The storehouse, still half full, was closed and gradually silence took the place of the brouhaha. I waited another hour. By now, only the water lapping against the *Medium*—also asleep—could be heard.

When I climbed through the window, my foot landed too hard on the metallic wall. The emptiness of the place and the quiet outside made the reverberations sound sinister. I waited. Silence.

A few moments later I was entering the other storeroom through the front door, left ajar as if they knew I was coming.

I'd never had to deal with a container before, and I had no idea how to open it. The crowbar I had in the sheath of my left pant leg—so heavy it was throwing me off balance—would have been about as useful as a toothpick. But the lantern was useful. I found the mechanism, which was simple but noisy as hell. I'm not sure whether I was sweating from the effort I was making or from the panic each sound produced. But the sailors of the *Medium* slept like logs, or maybe my ears had suddenly become super-sensitive.

Boxes of wood, just like at Gòmara's factory. Now the crowbar was useful.

My hand and the lantern brushed the length of the planks inside, while I reflected that the exchange of woods didn't make any sense at all—Filipino wood here, Catalan wood there... Meantime, I knew by both the look and the feel that it wasn't eucalyptus. I moved the lever again. Inside the boxes, I discovered not what I was looking for, but something much more delicate, completely protected by layers of metal and artificial cork.

Gòmara Wood labeled the big wooden boxes. I took a strip of one of the planks and a piece of what was inside the lined boxes. I was so disconcerted I wasted precious time trying to decide whether to close that container and open another one to see if I would find what I had really come to look for. I finally decided to be sensible; I reclosed the container I'd opened so that no one could possibly tell that anyone had tampered with it.

But when I started to repeat the operation on another container, I cursed the care I'd used a moment earlier. Because I heard a voice from outside, and this time it wasn't my hypersensitive ears playing tricks on me.

I put out the lantern and ran to the door, the spray ready in my left hand and the electric poker in my right, my heart a bundle of trembling fluff in my throat.

But the voices went by and died down along the docks.

I was going back to the second container when a siren went off, leaving me immobilized. And the yell that made my hair stand on end also made me decisive; I had to get out of there. I couldn't stay another second. What the hell was I doing in this bramble bush anyway?

As I left the storeroom, a light the level of a man's hand was dancing along the aisle formed by two rows of containers left outside. A lamppost lengthened the shadows of the two dawdling guards.

I hid; getting in so easily didn't mean I'd get out.

When I did get outside, it was already starting to get light. My heart dropped when two sailors suddenly appeared. They were drunk and the surprise made them laugh at first. Then they started yelling and causing an uproar that could have woken up the contents of all the containers on all the docks in the world. But the electric poker left them temporarily out of commission and mute. Just enough time for me to run, caution to the wind, towards the highway on Can Tunis.

Sunday

"Quim, I need you!"

"Lònia, for the love of God, it's Sunday!"

"That's just why I need you."

Sunday was a good day to follow someone. I'd decided to turn Gòmara's trail over to the antique dealer, but not to lose sight of her after I'd given her the information.

"Why the hell don't you follow her yourself?"

"I'll take the night shift. That way you can sleep and tomorrow you'll be fresh as a daisy for another mission."

I had to insist, but he finally agreed to meet me at the Plaça

Reial at eleven for an aperitif. Then I called the antique dealer and made a date with her at the same bar at twelve.

You couldn't take a step on the Rambla. It seemed like no one was going to the beach, but in Barcelona there were plenty of people to go around.

I bought a pot with a geranium in bloom and then watched the people coming and going from Virreina Hall. I hadn't been inside a museum or seen an exhibit for ages. I used to enjoy that a lot, but with this heat, who would go in?

I got as far down as Santa Mònica, but the mugginess and pushing and shoving were just as bad as farther up. I poked around the stalls of trendy knickknacks a little, bought a pair of earrings with inlaid work, and headed towards the Plaça Reial, swearing I'd never again come downtown on a summer Sunday unless I was in dire straights.

Quim was already there, hiding behind an enormous mug of beer.

"You're straight out of the jaded sixties, kid."

"How about less bullshit and more explanations?"

I began at the beginning. He bawled me out paternally for last night's solitary adventure and grumbled like an old fart when I told him what I wanted him to do.

"... and don't lose sight of her. I'll be home and you can call me anytime. If there's nothing new, I'll relieve you at ten tonight. You go to the Gòmara factory tomorrow morning, early. Ask for a job, or whatever, but get inside. Talk to people. Find out what the hell they're exporting. But don't believe anything they tell you. Get inside the storeroom I was in and search the place. And try to get my poor car back."

"How do I know which storeroom you were in?"

"Wait, I'll draw you a map. Listen, be careful, Quim. And no matter what happens, call between one and two at the office. Okay?"

I drew from memory the factory building and the location of the storerooms, and we didn't have any more time to talk because it was getting close to noon.

"Now, go sit at a nearby table and when we separate, don't lose Gaudí."

She showed up right on time. She wasn't wearing makeup and she looked like she'd just gotten up. She looked younger when she wasn't trying to look so serious, and she was more cordial than ever.

I wrote down his name, address, the name of the factory, the telephone number I'd memorized in Gòmara's living room and the number at the factory I'd gotten off the invoices, all on a sheet of paper from my notebook. I even drew her a map.

"Doesn't he have an office in Barcelona?" she asked.

"Not that I've been able to find out about."

"Okay I'll get going," she said with a smile.

She seemed another person. I think it was the first time I'd seen her smile.

"You should make an appointment," I suggested. "You might find out that they won't let you in."

"Why?"

"See this side road? I marked the map with an X. Right here there's a car hidden that appears out of nowhere and intercepts pretty girls."

She looked dumbfounded. I went on,

"It's clear that Mr. Gòmara's traffic in stolen works of art is of some magnitude and his property is very well protected."

She looked like a kid who'd been caught telling a lie, and then it turns out that the lie is true.

"Have you been at his house yourself?"

"Yes, ma'am. It's horrendous how many works of art he has. And all the storerooms in the factory are full of raw materials to produce modernist wooden statues."

"What do you mean?" she wrinkled her brow.

"Nothing. Just be careful."

She looked around indifferently, putting the papers into her purse.

"What about the other one?" she finally said.

"The photographer is still taking pictures."

I glanced at Quim, signalling with my eyes. Then I looked at her. She held my gaze for a second and then shook her head so that her face was covered by hair.

A thousand questions were burning in my mouth. But I gulped down some orange juice. I didn't want her to suspect that I suspected, or to figure out that I knew a lot more than she could imagine. But I wondered how an apparently intelligent woman could believe that I hadn't discovered at least some of what she was trying to hide. Maybe she though I was a dummy, or crazy. But the time would come for a showdown between her and me.

And the fact is that I liked her, in spite of everything.

She got up, shaking my hand. I watched her until she disappeared behind the arcades, with Quim right behind her.

The evening was calm, but I was kind of annoyed. Mercè and I were still hanging on Sebastiana's indecision, her fears, her overwhelming burden, her mood swings. Euphoric, then depressed; black, then white. At home the fan, undaunted, kept going around insistently. Mercè's sermons were completely reasonable and sensible, but I knew them by heart and they were a pain, especially delivered in one long session.

Quim showed no signs of life. That meant Guadí was waiting until tomorrow to contact Gòmara. It also meant that I'd have to stay up all night and that tomorrow I'd need Neus' help.

In the late afternoon I took a little nap in advance and at nine I started to prepare for my shift. Mercè gave me the keys to her car and the news that Sebastiana had decided to have an abortion and that tomorrow she would go to the clinic to get the process started.

Sebastiana seemed calm and relieved. I gave her a kiss as I left.

"She came right home and didn't go out again," said Quim. "What a heavy Sunday, man!"

"That's how the job is, honey. Remember, call tomorrow between one and two."

I had a couple of cups of coffee at the place across the street from Gaudí's shop, secretly cursing myself: I'd come down here with the idea of spending the night in the car, parked on that street. But that street was blocked off to traffic, and I hadn't even noticed it until now. How many times had I come to that shop? How was it possible I hadn't noticed that detail? I felt like a failure, a fool. If I'd asked Gaudí how her clerk could have taken down the three guys' license numbers on a street where there was no traffic, I would have taken her fabrication apart from the beginning and I wouldn't be in the prickly pear patch I was in now.

But since mistakes are worse if you let them get to you, I took advantage of the night and made a very illegal maneuver. I brought the car in anyway and parked it, if not exactly in front of the shop, at one end of the street where I would watch the door of the apartment.

A whole night of silence and solitude is a long time.

Monday morning

"Lònia, I have a photo report to do today, and I'm way behind. They're starting to complain at the magazine that I'm not getting things done on time."

"Neus, don't forget you have that job at the magazine thanks to me. If you leave me in the lurch, you might end up there too."

"You don't need to threaten me, Lònia, I'll come."

"Okay. Sorry."

She got there just as someone was pulling up the blinds in the shop windows. The employee was already waiting outside. I told Neus what I wanted her to do, and then I went to move the car. But not without having to argue with a policeman.

I wish I'd never done that! Arguing with a cop about a car parked in the wrong place, which isn't yours anyway, and when you don't have your driver's license is a form of suicide. Especially early on Monday morning when people seem like they've just had vinegar for breakfast instead of coffee.

So I ended up at the police station, calling Mercè in desperation. When she confirmed that she had voluntarily let me use her car, the problem was that I didn't have any papers, and if my purse had been stolen, why hadn't I reported it to the police, and anyhow, why had I been carrying the real documents with me instead of photocopies, and besides how did they know whether I was really a detective, etc., etc. I had to ask Mercè to go to the office and get my license and my business papers, but then, how could I prove I was the same person whose name was on those documents?

"But don't you know any traffic cops who'll back you up?" Mercè asked. "Because you're not going to get out of this one."

I did know someone, but he was in a different department. The two of us left the station half an hour later, but then I had to put up with Mercè's dressing down. What was I waiting for to report the robbery, or loss, for that matter? Going around without documents was like a rabid dog going around without even a collar, and besides, she couldn't let me have her car any more.

"Please, Mercè... "

"What are you waiting for—to get yours back? Rent one, shit!"

"I can't go back to Gòmara's to get mine. And I can't rent one without a driver's license."

Mercè was a good kid. She gave me 24 hours to use her car, as long as I got my papers in order... which meant that either Quim would have to get my car back, or I'd have to go see my friend the policeman so he'd cut through the red tape and help me replace all my lost documents, without having to fill out all the forms.

But that morning all I had time to do was drop her off at her office and take the sample I'd gotten from the Medium to be analyzed at the lab. Then I had to rush to the office; it was one p.m. on the dot.

The telephone was ringing off the hook.

"Lònia... "

Damn that Sebastiana!

"What's up. Hurry, I'm expecting a call... "

"Listen, can't you go with me to Mercè's office? I'm scared to go there by myself."

"What do you think they're going to do to you, draw and quarter you?" She didn't answer; she was crying. "What's wrong now? Yesterday you had your mind made up and you seemed fine!" More silence. "Okay, I'll go with you. What time?"

"Four o'clock."

"Fine. I'll come by and get you. How are you feeling?"

"Real dizzy and I've been vomiting. You'll come for sure?"

"Yes, yes, I'll be there," and I hung up.

There was another call immediately. It was Neus. There hadn't been any action at all, except the clerk who went out for

111

coffee. Not even a customer. And she was tired of playing the fool.

"How long do I have to stay here?"

"Give me the number at the bar. I'll let you know by two."

I hung up and thought how odd it was that Gaudí still hadn't contacted Gòmara. Maybe she had, by telephone . . . Mine rang again.

"This is Quim."

"What's up?"

"I'm at the police station."

"What's a nice guy like you doing in a place like that?"

"No shit, Lònia. I've been arrested for robbery."

"Have you gone crazy?"

He didn't say anything. Neither did I.

"Are you coming, or what?" His voice sounded far away.

"Yes, of course. But what happened?"

"You wouldn't want me to tell you over the phone. Listen, my ID card is at home. I was carrying a photocopy, but they took it, so now besides the robbery I have no documentation."

"That makes two of us. What a mess."

"You'll have to go by my place. The doorwoman has the key."

I'd never been to his place. I wish I'd had more time so I could have poked around a little. You learn a lot about a person from their house. In the few minutes I was there, I noticed that everything looked nice and neat. He had a lot of plants with lush, shiny leaves. Who took care of them when he did his disappearing act, I wondered?

I could tell by the way my policeman friend greeted me that his crush on me was still good for something, and I took advantage of it. In exchange for a date to go out for dinner whenever I wanted to, and could—what might happen later was unforeseeable and I couldn't be bothered worrying about it at the moment—he promised to do everything he could to help me get duplicates of my papers with a minimum of hassles. All I had to do was sign a form reporting that my purse had been snatched right on Passeig de Gràcia on Sunday at two in the afternoon, and sign forms for each document I needed—which could all be done right in his office. He didn't hide his professional pride, showing me how diligently his orders were followed. I felt like I'd found my fairy godmother—he even got me out of my mess with the traffic cops.

He even signed papers himself so they'd let Quim go.

"If he's working for you, as you say, then there must be some mistake," he smiled with self-satisfaction, "or maybe we overreacted."

I left the station as if I'd seen miracles. It had all been too good to be true. And since I still didn't quite believe it, I didn't want to break the spell by questioning the way they'd arrested me. I didn't want to get greedy only to find myself back at square one again.

"How did you do it?" Quim asked me. "What did you tell them?"

"Nothing. I didn't need to explain anything. Just connections."

"That guy that shook my hand is your sweetie?"

"Don't be an idiot, Quim. He did me a favor, that's all. Now tell me what happened."

"Not much. I was waiting for Mr. Llofriu, the guy in charge, to see me. In the meantime, I started chatting with some workers... They told me that they brought wood in from the Philippines and made furniture with it, most of which was exported."

"To the Philippines?"

"Among other places. As a matter of fact, Gòmara does do business in the Philippines. All quite legal."

"Go on."

"When I went into Llofriu's office, guess who was right behind me?"

"I'm not up for guessing games."

"The two cops. They had handcuffs on me before I could make a peep. Inside the car, the one with the eyebrows stuck a pistol in my hand—not a regulation one, and the car wasn't a police car either—and told me, nicely, that they'd just arrested me for attempted armed robbery."

"So you couldn't get into the storeroom or get my car back?"

"No, but I did find out something very interesting."

"Let's have it."

"Gòmara had a heart attack, the workers told me. They took

him to the clinic this morning by ambulance."

My stream of questions stopped. I drove mechanically for a while, until Quim's voice kept me from running into the car in front of me, stopped at a red light. I thought of poor Neus, who must still be watching Gaudí's store. My stomach felt empty, and I remembered that I'd not only not slept, I hadn't eaten either. I looked at the sky and all I could see was that the street lights were on and the shops lit up too.

"Quim, are you sure the antique dealer didn't leave her house yesterday?"

"Of course I'm sure! Go on, get lost! What's wrong with you, Lònia?"

I stopped the car as soon as I could and looked for a phone booth. I had Quim get out of the car and go substitute for Neus at the bar.

"But what the hell's going on, Lònia?"

"Don't ask stupid questions, shit!"

"Hello Mercè? You've got to find out for me where they took Ernest Gòmara this morning. He had a heart attack."

"What about Sebastiana?"

Sebastiana! I'd promised I'd go with her at four.

"She didn't show up?"

"No, and nobody answers at your house."

"The hell with her! I have a job to do and I can't be hanging around waiting for her to shit or get off the pot. And I'm not a babysitter. She'll go tomorrow, or if she's changed her mind, she'll have to lie in the bed she's made. Listen, get that information for me now, Merceneta, and call me at the office right away."

XIII

I'd been dozing off and on for about two hours when Mercè called.

"He's at the Garbí Clinic. He didn't pull through. They took him out of intensive care at five this afternoon."

"Do you know anyone at the clinic?"

"Yes, Berta . . . she's the one who told me that."

"Is she there now?"

"She's on call. Why?"

"Can I trust her?"

"You can trust all the women in my group."

"Listen, call her again and tell her I'll be right there. Tell her to help me out and not to ask questions."

"Listen, Lònia, don't you think you're pretty demanding of your friends?"

"Come on, Mercè. No sermons now."

No one was at the clinic office at the moment, but Berta Prat was very nice, and besides she had the keys. We had no trouble finding not only Gòmara's file, but also his death certificate, signed by Dr. Andreu Canal, director and owner of the clinic.

"Can you check and see if Felip Antal's file is here too?"

It was a sudden hunch, and it turned out to be brilliant one. The file was there, too. He had been brought in in a deep coma as the result of an accident. His death certificate had also been signed by Dr. Canal.

"Is he the one who signs all the death certificates?"

"Actually, the director of each department should sign, and

115

this one belongs in trauma. But if it was an emergency, and the department director wasn't on call . . . "

"So you mean it's not unusual."

"It's not normal, but not really unusual either."

"I assume Gòmara's body is still at the clinic?"

"I don't know. We can look in the morgue."

Berta was a jewel. But the morgue was closed, and she didn't have the key for it.

"This is really weird," she said. "The morgue never closes. People don't die on schedule. I'll ask about it."

"No, don't do that, Berta. If it's closed, it's because there's something in there somebody doesn't want anybody to see. Will you let me play a little trick?"

She let me. Looking very serious and professional, I used my wits and a hairpin while the doctor looked on, curious and surprised.

When we went into the morgue—how cool it was in there!—she made a joking comment, but her face froze when I pulled back the shroud.

Maybe it had been a heart attack, but caused by something very heavy that had crushed him between the waist and the knees.

Needless to say, Berta Prat put herself totally at my disposal, not because of Mercè's friendship any more; out of principle now.

First of all, I asked her to get me an appointment to talk to Dr. Canal, and then permission for Neus to do a photographed report of the clinic.

"I'll call to set up the day and time," I said as we walked through the garden. "Don't let on that you know anything."

The bar had closed hours ago. Quim was waiting for me sitting in a doorway, like a drunk. But when I told him to come with me to see Gaudí, he came through.

"This isn't the time to go visiting, Lònia!"

"It's exactly the right time."

It was four in the morning. The door to the building was locked, and there was no outside buzzer. I sent Quim to call from a booth.

"Tell her I'm down here and not to keep me waiting. And come right back."

But before he got back, Gaudí had peeked out the window and was rushing down to open the door.

"What's going on?" her voice was rough and her eyes murky.

"That's what you're going to tell me," I said, pushing her towards the stairway without further ado.

She turned around and looked at me after a few steps. Now there was fear in her eyes instead of surprise.

"It's four in the morning!"

I pushed her up the stairs again. When we were inside her apartment, I closed the door and said,

"What I don't understand is why you haven't made your getaway yet. You've got a lot of nerve! Do you take me for an idiot, or do you think you can get away with anything?"

"What are talking about? What's this all about?"

"How did you do it? When? Where? Who helped you?"

She seemed about to crack for a second, but then she recovered immediately, as if by magic, turning back into the woman I'd first met. She had me come in, and for a second I thought I was dreaming. The apartment was incredible. It was a magnificent palace, extravagant and welcoming, that was hidden away on that dark little street. I'd loved to have snooped around a little, if I hadn't been in such a hurry. But Gaudí indicated a sofa to me that looked like it had been previously owned by the King of France.

"Would you like something to drink?" she asked, sure of herself and everything around her.

"Milk."

I followed her into the kitchen. She was wearing a satin crepe robe in its natural off-white color, embroidered around the shoulders, just like the godmother of the rich kid in my home town.

"Gòmara's dead," I said.

I didn't think my straightforwardness would have such an effect. Besides being a storyteller, she was also a perfect actress who could effectively handle such tricks as looking astounded and quick changes in expression. Some of the milk missed the glass and dribbled down to the floor, a drop at a time. She looked at the spilled milk, and then at me and then at the milk, and then at me again.

"But... but... I just saw him Sunday," she stuttered.

Now I was the one who had to control my expressions. Lucky Quim hadn't come up. Lucky for him, of course. Imbecile, dumbshit Quim, idiot!

"Naturally you saw him. And you killed him... "

"That's not true!"

I started yelling at her. I took her by the wrist and led her back into the living room. I pushed her onto the King's sofa she had just offered me. When I had her cornered, I gave her a couple of good slaps.

"No, no, Miss Guiu... I'll tell you everything."

"Why didn't you come upstairs?" I asked Quim, who was waiting for me at the door.

"It was locked. Did you find out anything?"

"Yeah, that you're an idiot, Quim."

He took a long look at his watch.

"I don't like compliments like that at five in the morning."

"And I don't like people who work for me to have their eyes on the wrong side of their heads. Where were you Sunday at three in the afternoon?"

He thought about it for a minute. Then he looked at me and started laughing:

"Here, in the bar, watching to see if she would go out."

"And no one went out, right? All day long, right, moron? Just for your information, Gaudí went right past you."

We'd gotten to the car. Quim got in, puzzled. When I got behind the wheel, he grabbed my hand. His eyes looked wild.

"Lònia... I didn't look at my watch because I thought... That door doesn't go anywhere but to her apartment? There aren't any other apartments? It's a two story building."

"What are you saying? What are you trying to excuse yourself for?"

"No, it's just that... Yes, a woman came out through that door. But it wasn't Gaudí! It was a dish that took your breath

118

away! Even the waiter came out to look at her. Tall, with high heels that made her ass wiggle, a dress cut so low you could practically see her belly button, what cleavage!"

"You're brainless, Quim. A real idiot!"

"Lònia, I swear it wasn't Gaudí. Impossible. Gaudí doesn't have boobs like that!"

"It was her, all right. And I told you from the beginning she was an attractive woman, but you didn't believe it."

"So she's the one who... "

"No. Or yes. But no, she couldn't have."

He was so cowed, and so embarrassed, that I had to forgive him. As we went up to his house, I explained the conversation I'd had with Gaudí.

She had telephoned Gòmara and explained who she was. But there was a slight variation on the first version. Otherwise, Gòmara wouldn't have come down to Barcelona to talk to her. They were a gang of exotic art smugglers. They robbed from tombs in India, Mexico, Panama, the Phillipines. Gaudí was a link in the chain. A broken link, one they had left out when she asked for more of a commission, and then tried to find out who they really were, what they had for a front. She had threatened to turn Gòmara in if he didn't come to talk to her, and he had come. And later today, she was supposed to meet with Gòmara and the third man, in her store. But of course, that meeting wouldn't take place.

"Did you believe all that?"

"In a way. What time did the magnificent lady come back?"

"Wait. It was late afternoon. An hour and a half or two later... "

"Later than what?"

"Later than the time she left. Lònia, if you'd told me that she was the only one who used that door... How was I supposed to know that that woman... "

"Forget it, Quim. It's done."

We had arrived at his house. Before he got out, he asked, "What are you going to do now?"

"Sleep, and we'll try again tomorrow. Good night."

I liked to drive at night in Barcelona, all alone. I felt in charge of things. That drive from Quim's, in Gràcia, to my place relaxed me by contrast: I hadn't felt in charge of anything. Gaudí could have killed both Gòmara and Antal just as easily as not. The stuff about smuggled art might be true and it might not be. Gaudí even had an answer for the scam about the clerk who was able to get the licence number in a street where cars weren't allowed: she had met with Antal, and she'd seen, of course, the license plate on his car.

I had the feeling something was a little off, like the clothes my older cousin gave me, which never quite fit. My mother was an expert seamstress, and she always made things over so they seemed made just for me. But she wasn't around any more.

Mechanically, I turned off the motor. I was dying to sleep. Tomorrow was another day. When the elevator got to my floor, I remembered about Sebastiana.

She was in the bathtub, which was filled to the top with water tinged with blood. With some vomit floating on top.

I grabbed hold of the door, as hard as I could. On the stool, there was a little glass and an empty bottle of valium. Razor blades on the floor. Everything you can think of, just in case, kid.

A grimace of disgust twisted her mouth, and a deep wrinkle between her brows were evidence of the physical pain. No pain now, of any kind.

A voice made me jump; it was my own, instinctively uttering every curse I knew, while my body was losing its physical consistency, and all sensations were fading away.

I reacted in midfall and ended up on my knees. I got up immediately and headed straight for the telephone.

"Quim! Quim! Come here, right away!"

And then:

"Mercè . . . come over . . . Sebastiana! Hurry up!"

They found me hanging on the door again, my eyes fixed on Sebastiana's wrinkled brow. I was dying to know what passed through her mind in the last moments, and if she held anything against me. My insides had melted away, and there wasn't anything left but my bones holding up my skin to keep up appearances. All the rest was a great vacuum—foggy and in pain, horribly guilty. I'd taken her in, and then left her so she could kill herself.

Somebody took me by the arms and led me to an armchair. Somebody else was talking on the phone.

What deep desperation had cornered her so that killing herself seemed the only way out? What nameless fears? What solitude?

"Are you related to her?" someone asked me in Spanish. I shook my head no.

"But she lived here, with you. Did she have any problems? Was she sick?"

"She had a worm in her belly," I heard myself say. I got up and they told me not to move. Someone grabbed me by the arm.

"Leave me alone!" I cried, wrenching my hand away.

"Leave her alone for a few minutes." It was Quim's voice in an unrecognizable accent. "She's blown away."

I started searching the house. Surely she'd left a note, something that would let me know what went through her head. There were eyes everywhere, looking at me, accusing me. I'd abandoned her, I hadn't helped her enough. When I reached for her purse, a voice said:

"Don't touch anything. We'll do it."

The flashes blinded me. I was sickened by the indecency of photographing her like that. But I didn't have the strength to complain. More people were coming. Unknown men kept going into the bathroom to violate Sebastiana all over again.

"Get out! Get out! Leave her alone for once!" I screamed. Quim kept me from throwing myself upon them, and once again took me by the arms and led me to the sofa.

"We'll have to call Majorca, Lònia," he was saying. "To have her parents come. You can't hold yourself responsible."

Mercè was talking to the investigator and the court pathologist. But the inspector kept insisting that I was the one who had to explain things. Before answering anything, I called Majorca.

"Is this Joana?"

"She's not here. Who is this?" It was the voice of an old woman.

"Is Pere there?"

"He's not here either. Who's calling?"

I looked at the clock: seven in the morning. Where could they be at this hour? They didn't work the fields any more.

"This is Lònia Guiu, a friend of Sebastiana's. I'd like to speak to them, Sebastiana's had an... "

"Oh, you're calling from Barcelona! What a coincidence! They took the boat to Barcelona last night."

"Did they call anyone?"

"They called Sebastiana! Is she there? Darling, it's your grandmother, that was so naughty, to run away like that...

I hung up. I looked around; my house was full of people, like a day at the fair.

The questions were a formality, and I answered them mechanically. The pathologist said benevolently that it wasn't the first time a pregnant girl had killed herself. But Sebastiana wasn't a pregnant girl any more; she was a dead body wrapped in gray plastic that two men were putting on a stretcher.

"Can you come here a minute?"

I followed the voice into the hallway. The whole house was a disaster area. Full of smoke, cigarette butts everywhere. A policeman was looking curiously at my lipstick collection, perfectly arranged in a glass case made especially for it.

"What's this?"

"Is this for the report, or just out of curiosity?"

"Both," he said gruffly.

"Lipstick. I collect them. It's a mania, like any other."

I looked at them. It had been a while since I'd examined them closely. I remembered each one, even the day and the place I'd bought it.

There was one I didn't recognize.

It was golden, and it even looked like gold, out of the case. It was a little bigger than the others, in a sort of container you'd carry it in your purse in. I never bought containers; I didn't like them. I opened it. There was no lipstick in it. Just a piece of paper, folded into a little wad.

"Dear Lònia, I spent all I had left to buy you this. It's a silly way to thank you for all your help, but my head isn't clear enough to think of anything better. Mom called. Jerònia gave her this number and told her I was pregnant. That I'd been raped and I wanted an abortion. She bawled me out. She called me a pig. She said she was coming to get me with Dad and that Dad would give me just what I deserved. They don't want to shame

122

the family. I can't explain how I feel. I'm afraid. But I also want to make them feel bad, I want to show them what shame is all about. I'd rather die. I got a bottle of valium to put myself to sleep so I can't change my mind. When I've taken all the pills, I'm going to slit my veins. I'll go to sleep while I'm bleeding. The only thing I'm sorry about is that I'll cause you a lot of trouble. Tell Mercè I'm sorry. And don't be mad at me for messing up your bathtub. Sebastiana."

If I'd only come by at four to pick her up like I'd promised, she'd be alive now, I screamed to myself silently. The screams knocked around inside my brain and came watering out my eyes, unstoppable. I gave the letter to Mercè.

"How awful," she said when she'd read it.

XIV

Wednesday

When Sebastiana's parents showed up and took charge of things, since they couldn't do otherwise, Mercè and Quim insisted that I take a break. The truth is that I didn't make them insist very much, because I didn't feel like doing anything and I couldn't enjoy anything.

A strong sedative, a comfortable bed at Mercè's house, a dark, quiet room; I slept like I had at Gòmara's after they'd hit me on the head—a whole day and night. I woke up without any physical pain, and the ache in my soul had let up enough for me to realize that life goes on. My life.

"You can keep using my car," Mercè said generously as we were having breakfast. And finally, "Berta called yesterday. She has some things for you."

I called her right away. She'd gotten permission for me to have the photo report done, any time I wanted. The interview with Dr. Canal would depend on his schedule, but she would try. However, she told me, when I tell you what I've found out, you might not think it's necessary.

I called Neus.

"Oh, Lònia," she said in her most moronic tone, "I'm working on a historical report . . . I'll be busy all day sorting photos from my file and tomorrow I'll have to develop them . . . "

"Neus . . . "

"I know, I know, you don't have to tell me again that if it wasn't for you . . . Will you help me organize the photos afterwards?"

"Sure. I'll meet you at the Garbí Clinic two hours from now."

124

"Lucky I didn't have this done officially," Joan said when he saw me. "If they'd put this in the register, I'd have been in a heap of trouble. Where'd you get this stuff?"

"What is it?"

"It's heavy stuff. I wrote up a technical report for you, and a layman's one you can understand," he handed me two sheets of paper a little the worse for wear from having been in his shirt pocket. "I wrote it at home. I don't want it to get mixed up with the laboratory stuff."

While I read the layman's report, Joan went to get the sample. He had it locked up in his desk drawer.

"What have you been up to, Lònia? This is dangerous stuff," he smiled. "No, I don't want to know. But my discretion has a price."

I realized it was the Cheshire cat's smile.

"What is it?"

"Well, for example, you could invite me to dinner at your place again without that hypocrite of a Majorcan around, and you could promise not to fall asleep . . . "

I'm sure his mother had no idea what an asshole she'd brought into the world. But I didn't say a word.

"Okay. We'll talk about it, sweetie," I said.

"We sure will, dear. I'll call you."

Now his smile looked like a pig's.

Berta Prat hung up the phone and wrote out permission for Neus to do the report on official stationery and in official language. She'd have to show it to each department head where she wanted to take pictures. But she knew we were mainly interested in men in their forties, balding, tall and fat, with drawn faces.

When Neus left, Berta had me sit down, smiling with satisfaction.

"I've found out some things. Don't worry, I was very discreet. Antal didn't die from an accident, he was castrated." Berta laughed, no doubt at my expression. "Isn't it something? Anyway, it turns out that Dr. Canal was a great pal of Antal, and even more of Antal's wife, and now they're even better, uh, friends. Seems they're going to get married. But it wasn't the

Baroness, or Canal, who castrated him." Berta was having a great time as a detective. "Turns out Antal gave a lot of business to whores, if you'll excuse the expression. He was involved in selling Filipino women, they say. Seems he stole the girlfriend of the guy who was procuring him the Filipino women, and the Filipino punished him. Dr. Canal, who was afraid all of Antal's shit would expose his relationship with the Baroness, made the report out saying it was an accident, and the Baroness went along with it, naturally... "

"And you didn't know a thing about all this?"

"I had no idea. It seems only certain people know—orderlies, watchmen, cleaning women. It's pretty clear the staff is out to lunch. Oh, and a detective, a friend of Antal's, came snooping around. But they assure me that he left as ignorant as he came. A guy named Arquer... "

"Lluís Arquer," I said. "That's what I figured. What kind of a guy is Dr. Canal?"

"You'll see yourself. Wait in the bar, and his secretary will let you know when he can see you for your so-called interview."

"How about Gòmara?"

"They cremated him yesterday."

"Have you heard any talk? Any rumors about him?"

"Not a word."

"You must have some security guards at this place. I haven't seen any... "

"Yes, I've seen some men in uniforms... especially in the lab and in the storeroom. A lot of drugs get stolen."

"What company is it? The security guards, I mean?"

"I have no idea. Do you want me to look it up?"

She looked it up. It was—what else?—the Rec company.

There weren't many people in the coffee shop. Background music. Since you could smoke there, everyone had a cigarette in their hand. Relatives who had taken boring visitors out of the sick person's room and were chatting around a table. Personnel in white or green lab coats standing at the counter.

The smell of coffee with milk gave me an uncontrollable desire to have an *ensaïmada* dipped in the coffee, early in the morning before I went to school. A fresh *ensaïmada*, straight from the oven in a big new basket mother had just gotten.

But I ordered a croissant.

"Miss Mireia Gual?"

I was so wrapped up in the croissant that I was about to say no to the white coat, with a girl inside, that had just come up and was leaning towards me.

"Yes," I said.

"Dr. Canal will see you now."

I ran into Neus in the hallway. She had just taken pictures of Dr. Canal and she was finished. We'd see each other at the magazine, she said, winking.

"Come in, Miss Gual."

He looked me over from head to foot, as if he were x-raying me. He was one of those men who was good-looking enough to take your breath away at first sight. On closer scrutiny, you saw he indeed fit the description of a classically handsome man down to the last detail, in spite of a bit of phoniness in his gestures and the way he dealt with you. Too handsome, too gorgeous to be a man, my mother would say. And too nice. One of those who would reach out to shake hands exaggeratedly, with a gesture that was meant to seem sincere but which always gave me the impression that they were trying to keep you at a distance.

We talked about how clinics really were, from the inside, about the research he was doing, private and public medicine, transplants, insemination, professional ethics... And when I was just about to get to the questions I was really interested in they called him on the intercom. He apologized, got up and said we'd have to finish the interview later. If I wanted, I could wait for him there.

I took advantage of it to snoop around. I wasn't looking for anything special... or maybe I was. In his library, full of tomes bound in leather, there was a medical dictionary. Inside that, a freight invoice that kept me from waiting for him.

I've never liked clinics, but that one didn't smell of disinfectant at all. I went into the linen room, and among the sheets, pajamas, and towels, I found a shelf with white lab coats and the hospital clogs left behind by some of the cleaning women. Just what I needed.

It was a big clinic, well marked. The lab didn't smell like a clinic, either. There was just a kid, busy with something at his desk. I looked at the jars, bottles and labels.

"Don't touch anything," the boy said distractedly. "What are you looking for?"

I didn't answer, obliging him to look at me.

"Are you new?"

"Yes."

I went up to him. There were a bunch of little bottles in a basket, the kind they have at flower shops. All empty. Next to him there was a sheet of paper with a list of names that were very familiar to me.

"What are you doing?" I asked. I leaned languorously over his back.

"You still haven't told me your name. Just wanted to know."

He had crossed his arms and turned the stool around. He was looking at me like a bacterium through a microscope. But he probably didn't have that malicious gleam in his eye when he looked through microscopes. You've got to be pretty bad to want to make it with bacteria.

I smiled complacently, but our idyll was interrupted by the arrival of one of the security men from Rec. He stuck his head through the door:

"Everything okay?" he asked the guy.

"Yeah, sure," he said quickly, and the man shut the door. Then the kid grabbed me around the waist. "I can't play around . . . now. What time do you get off?"

"How about you?"

We made a date. I left the lab wiggling my hips a lot. At the door, I winked at the security guard and walked down the hall, very slowly.

It took me a while to find the storage room. It was in the second basement, not marked like all the other departments. It was closed, but there was a light on inside. Through the porthole I could see a man sitting at a desk, and a little further down, another guy in a Rec uniform taking a nap.

I called the central office on the inside line from the telephone in the hall.

"Who's in the storeroom, Miss?"

128

It took her a few moments to answer. When she told me the name, I asked to be connected with him.

"Mr. Pere, Dr. Canal wants you both to come upstairs immediately," I said.

"Right away."

I ran to the elevator and went up to the first floor. I waited in the hallway. The elevator went back down right away and came back up with Mr. Pere and the guard. Then I went back down.

The storeroom door resisted both my wit and the hairpin. I trusted that it would take a while for Mr. Pere and his pal to find Dr. Canal, and that Dr. Canal wouldn't have the building thoroughly searched for me.

The lock finally gave way. The storeroom was enormous. Even if they kept all the drugs for all the clinics in Barcelona, it was still too big. Did the sick people in that place consume that much shit?

I worked quickly. I had time to see just about everything I had expected. But just as I was about to grab a little bottle as proof, I heard the elevator door. As I put the bottle in the pocket of my lab coat, the storeroom door opened and the volume of the voices increased, because they'd found the lock jimmied. They spread out along the aisles formed by metallic shelving and through the passageways lined with boxes and cans.

I tried to figure out how many people there were and to localize them by their voices, but before I could do that a sinister and dangerous silence fell. I heard some steps and a curse nearby, and I took the risk; leaving the clogs behind, I ran towards the door barefooted. I saw the guard who'd come into the lab through some scantily filled shelves. Dr. Canal was at the door, alarm wrinkling his brow. The guard was coming towards me, but he still hadn't seen me. I grabbed a can from a shelf and threw it as far away from myself as I could. The guard turned and went towards the racket. Dr. Canal went to the desk, leaving the door ajar. They were making it easy for me. I kept on walking among the obstacles, and by the time they'd found my clogs, I was out of there.

I went up the stairs so I wouldn't give myself away with the elevator. But when I started to get off at the first floor, I saw the same two types who had threatened to take my license away coming towards me hurriedly and looking uneasy. So I went back to the stairs and went up to the next floor. Department of Gynecology and Obstetrics. But a security guard was just entering Berta's office.

I went towards the elevator, then to the service elevator. I stood beside a stretcher on wheels, pulled by an orderly. Inside, he asked me where I'd lost my shoes. But the door to the first floor was already opening and I left without answering him.

I went out through the garden in the rear, running like a maniac. By the time I got to the car, my feet were destroyed.

But I didn't want to go home. Without realizing it, I'd gotten used to knowing that I'd find Sebastiana there. Now just thinking about the emptiness I knew would be waiting for me filled me with pain.

I found Quim at the office.

"Your friend the policeman called, and he has all the documents, or at least the certificates for them . . . What happened to you? Where did you leave your shoes?"

My very own guardian angel was a doting mother; he'd even installed a first aid kit in the new office. As I was washing off my feet with rusty water:

"*Pink and Blue* called, too. The director is furious; two cops have been there twice now, asking for two different people, but he suspects they're both you."

"They'll be back soon. How the hell did they know the telephone number there? Damn that Neus!"

"Your cop friend knew it too."

"I gave it to him. The people at the magazine didn't tell those pigs anything, did they?"

"No, but if they pressure him, he will, the director told me to tell you. I told him they were just two dopes moonlighting and they couldn't do anything but hassle him. He didn't seem convinced at all."

When Quim went down to the shopping center to get me some shoes and a cheese sandwich—another day without eating except for the croissant at lunchtime—I called the magazine. I got a few days' truce in exchange for the news about the future wedding and past affair of Dr. Canal and the Baroness of Prenafeta. Then I called Joan at the lab.

"Just tell me whether the sample Quim is going to bring you is the same substance as the one I brought in . . . the pay will be double, Joan—two dinners."

"How about a tip?"

"Okay, a tip, too."

Pig.

Then I called my policeman friend. And finally Neus.

"I'll come as soon as I eat. Do you want Quim to come and help us with the photos too?"

My cop friend took me to dinner at the breakwater. The smell of refried oil was overwhelming. The tables were dirty and the windows facing the sea were all misted over. The music at full blast made us yell rather than talk.

He may have advanced in rank, but he still hadn't cleaned up his act. If he thought he was going to seduce me in that atmosphere, he had another thought coming. But he'd given me the new documents and I had to be nice to him. I did refuse, no matter how much he insisted, to eat seafood. Just a salad and yogurt.

While he was paying, I went out to look at the sea. Black as could be. Sparkling with fishing boats with lights. I missed Majorca. I decided that when I was finished with this case, I'd go for a week or two. And I'd take some flowers to Sebastiana's grave.

"Where do you want to go now?" he'd grabbed me by the shoulder and I got a whiff of 'Varon Dandy.' He was a real tacky type, all right. I was sick to death of men who always want the same thing in exchange for any favor they do for you. "Do you want to go dancing?"

"I'm sorry, but I promised a friend I'd help her with a job she has to have done for tomorrow."

"But . . . but I thought . . . " his Spanish was pretty rough, just like when he used to moonlight in the department stores.* His upward mobility had been really superficial.

"Yes, I know the price of the favor you did for me is higher."

"It has nothing to do with prices, Lònia . . . "

"Of course it does. That's what we agreed. I understand per-

---

* Most officials speak Castilian, even in Catalonia.

fectly the half words and insinuations. But today I can't do it. Sorry."

"Some other time?"

"Sure."

I thought about the guy at the clinic lab, who was probably still waiting for me with the same thing on his mind. I couldn't help laughing.

You could see the towers of Sagrada Familia through the pasty fog from Neus' attic apartment. I felt a tickle going up my spine. Maybe I'd taken a chill at the breakwater after the sticky mugginess of the bar.

"Do you have anything for a headache? Not aspirin, though."

"I thought vegetarians didn't take medicine."

"Female ones do."

Photos were scattered on a table that ran the entire length of a wall. Quim was already at work, happy as a dog with a new bone. When Neus had explained how to sort them and given us the magnifying glass so we could see the proofs better, she shut herself up in the lab to develop the stuff from the clinic.

"What did Joan from the lab say?" I asked Quim before I got started.

"You can drop by tomorrow."

I was blinking, my headache had come back, and the arranging job was driving me crazy. I'd been looking at proofs for two hours and marking down on a piece of paper the numbers of the references I was sorting. Neus was very organized. With my list and Quim's, she'd be able to find the negatives right away and blow them up. Outdoor weddings, kids feeding pigeons in the plazas of Barcelona, groups of young people throwing money around, boy scouts getting into buses, seafood stalls at the Barceloneta, men walking their dogs, people drinking from modernist fountains, old-timers playing petanca or bocci. Bucolic city scenes. Gypsies begging, kids passing joints around, men grabbing ass in the bus and the metro stations—how could Neus have taken all those pictures? To tell the truth, Neus was more of a professional than I'd thought—old men sleeping in portals and the metro stairs. The other side of city life. *Pink and Blue* wouldn't want those ones. Too pinko. And too damn good.

What I had in my hands was a bunch of worthless proofs. Dinners, night clubs, social ceremonies, conferences, all kinds of celebrations. I went through them quickly. But suddenly I cried out, jolting Quim.

"What's wrong?"

I passed the magnifying glass over that sheet of proofs, swearing without realizing it. The hair on my arms was standing on end.

"Get Neus!"

It was a big salon. Surely in a deluxe hotel. Round tables with men sitting around. The dinner half eaten. General views, partial views. Here a waiter blocking half the view. There half a table with men toasting. More partial views. More general views from other angles. A row of waiters in battle formation. The president's table with a bouquet of tulips on it. All men. Not a single woman. Dressed fit to kill. Black tie and shiny lapels.

At one of the tables, Gòmara and Antal were sitting right next to each other.

"Look at this, Neus. Tell me it's true. Tell me!"

"Good grief! The two dead men!"

"Let me see!" said Quim.

Neus put the proofs into the amplifying apparatus. We found Dr. Canal at another table. And the Filipino dressed in white next to him, and Martí, the one from the factory, in a guard's uniform standing by the dining room door.

"Where was this?" I asked, impatiently. "When? Neus, blow them all up for me, quick, as big and detailed as you can. This time we've got them for sure!"

I was furious I hadn't looked at these photos earlier. They say there aren't any coincidences in this job. From now on, people who say that will have to think twice.

Neus went back and closed herself up in the lab with the negatives. I took notes on the information from the cards with the corresponding number and the letters on the sets of proofs. Quim had gone into the kitchen to fix a warm bite to eat.

It had been one of those nights like we used to have at the

apartment, when my roommates were taking exams. And just like after those all-nighters, I had a cup of tea in the morning and went to sleep like a log, on the floor, with a cushion under my head and a newspaper covering my face.

XV

Thursday morning

The contents of the little bottle from the Garbí Clinic were, in fact, the same as those found in the identical bottle from the Gòmara Factory. To celebrate, I went to a perfume store on the upper part of Rambla de Catalunya and bought the most expensive lipstick they had.

Then I went down to the cathedral plaza and, still celebrating, parked in the parking garage behind the College of Architecture.

By mid-morning I was entering the antique shop with a file full of photos. The ones from the clinic and the blow-ups.

Gaudí had me come into the shop's office and started looking them over slowly. When she'd gone over about half of them, she seemed bored, tired of it. But I made her go on. She stopped when she got to the president's table. She pointed out, not too decisively, one of the seated men. I looked through the rest of the photos and found the close-up. Neus had done a good job, and quick.

"Yes, that's him," said Gaudí.

"Are you sure?"

"Positive."

He had white hair with a receding hairline. His face was drawn, but he didn't look fat at all. And he was older than the other two.

"You're absolutely sure it's him?"

She said yes with no hesitation, and some rage in her voice.

"When was this taken?" she asked.

"The fifteenth of May."

She made a sort of exclamation, like a grunt.

"Are you okay?"

"Yes, yes," she wiped off her forehead. "It's hot in here, don't you think?"

"You don't recognize anyone else in the other pictures? Nobody looks familiar?"

"No, not at all," she paused. "I only had contact with those three, out of the whole organization."

"Two of them died when I found them . . . ."

Gaudí shrugged her shoulders, then wiped her forehead again. I collected all the photos and left the store, determined I would find the third man that very day.

At the hotel, they sent me to public relations. I realized as soon as I went in, the way they looked at me in my blue jeans and striped shirt not tucked in, that it was one errand I should have gotten dressed up for. Too late. I was already there and I didn't plan to return.

"What do you want to know for?" the executive's voice was suspicious and haughty. I got nervy.

"Is it some kind of a secret?"

"No, of course not, but as you can understand, we don't give information to just anyone who comes in asking for it."

"Okay, it's your loss," I headed for the door.

"Wait, Miss, you don't have to get mad . . . "

"I'm a reporter and I'm doing a story about Barcelona as a host of Fairs and Congresses. I know your hotel is state of the art for things like that. But if you withhold the information from me . . . don't complain later. If you want references for me, you can call *Pink and Blue*, even though the report is for the Frankfurt magazine *Neue Blume*. Well," I said with the door already open. "I don't like people to throw monkey wrenches into the works on me. I'm a professional and I know other places I can get information. I don't hide things, though, and I'd have to say you didn't treat me very well."

The executive started to mumble excuses. Reaching out towards me, he gently led me by the elbow to the armchair and had me sit down. He offered me cigarettes, and then a drink, which I refused. He placed everything I might want at my disposal.

"I just want to know what conferences and meetings have taken place here during the last trimester."

On May fifteenth, an international symposium on the care and maintenance of museums had celebrated its closing session. According to the hotel's information, it had been organized by the Goldsmith Museum Foundation, and sessions had been held in rooms at the Bar Association.

I found out at the Association that the rooms had been rented by the International Organization for Museums, affiliated with Art Mundial, which had a branch in Barcelona.

The office I went to looked like a charitable organization, Third Worldish. The people there didn't know what I was talking about.

"Wait," a guy said. "Jordi probably knows about it. Wait a minute."

He called Jordi on the phone, and gave me his address. Jordi was handicapped, and yes, he remembered that symposium perfectly. Mr. Pierre Jovel, curator of the Museum of Marais, in Lyon, had presided. Mr. Jovel was also the president of the IOM, and member of the executive council of the Goldsmith Foundation.

I showed him the pictures. Mr. Pierre Jovel was the third man.

Maybe that whole story about smuggling objets d'art was true after all. Maybe Gaudí hadn't told me as many lies as I thought. But why hadn't she told me the third man was French? Such an important clue!

"He's a big personality in the museum world," the guy in the wheelchair was telling me. "He comes to Barcelona a lot and spends summers on the Costa Brava, at Begur, I think. And he has a house in Pedralbes."

"What's your connection with Jovel?"

"The Foundation has a charitable section. They give scholarships to the handicapped, for studying and travelling. The people who work there are handicapped, for the most part. I'm a member of Cidob and they send me jobs once in a while. Art Mundial told us they were putting on this conference, and that the Foundation's policy is to give work to the handicapped. So I was in charge of all of the organization of the conference, under the direction of the big shots, as it were."

"Listen, aren't all those initials and organizations a big pain?"

"What do you mean, a pain?" But he knew what I meant, to judge by the expression on his face.

"A hassle."

"Well, they're organizations that operate under the auspices of UNESCO and some private organizations that collaborate from time to time. Sometimes, even though they're international, they have a different name in each country. You get used to it when you deal with it all the time."

"Did they pay you a lot for running the symposium?"

"A fortune! I was able to have my apartment made handicap-accessible. Now it's a model place for people like me."

"What kind of person is Mr. Jovel?"

"He's an excellent person."

Without even asking me what I wanted the information for, and without even a shadow of distrust, Jordi gave me the benefactor Pierre Jovel's address and telephone number in Barcelona. He not only didn't ask indiscreet questions, he didn't even ask for anything in return.

I felt bad about it for him: he would surely lose his golden egg because of me. But things aren't always the way we'd like them to be.

When I went outside, I realized it was a splendid day. The air was cool for a July day, and the setting sun had lost its midday punch.

I decided I had borrowed Mercè's car for too long, and that I could allow myself the luxury of renting one for a few days. At least until I got mine back. I felt rich; Gaudí would soon have to pay me what she owed me, and that was a lot. For the job I'd done and for the lies—or half-truths—I'd put up with. Not that I was planning to blackmail her, not that I was thinking of having her pay for my silence. I didn't want to keep my mouth shut. That was too much dirt to sweep under my rug.

There were still some loose threads to tie together, though. I wanted to know for sure what was inside the eucalyptus boxes at Gòmara's place. To touch it with my own hands. In the end, there was only one thing it could be. I wanted to find out for sure whether the story about Canal and the Baroness and the jealous

Filipino was true. And what connection there was between Jovel and the two dead men, besides the ones I suspected. More than anything I was curious how much was true about the art smuggling operation.

Jovel's presence resurrected that whole question, which I'd thought was a smoke screen.

I stopped at a cafe for an almond nectar. I called the office from a booth on the corner.

"Quim, I left Mercè's car in the garage on Muntaner, next to the Ninot. Go get it and return it to her. I'm going to rent one."

"Mercè called. She wanted to know what the hell you did at the Garbí Clinic. They fired Berta. And the magazine people have had more visitors."

It seemed like the whole day's mugginess was concentrated inside the booth. And the thick nectar was too heavy to get down.

"Shit! And everything was going so well today."

As a consolation, I bought myself another lipstick. But the problems weren't over. They're like a bowl of cherries, once you get started ... The vouchers for my documents weren't good enough for the car rental place. And my explanation that they'd stolen my car with the documents inside—perfectly plausible, after all—didn't convince them. After arguing with half the population, I decided there were other car rental agencies and as I was telling the guys at the desk to go fly a kite, I heard a happy voice behind me, yelling:

"Apol.lònia!"

It was Martí, the guy who used to live in the apartment on Plaça del Pedró. Rosa's ex. The fair-haired boy of the Economics faculty.

We hugged, and he gave me a big kiss. The guys at the desk dropped their teeth.

"What are you doing here? How's your life?"

"How about you?"

"Working in an office, as you can see ... "

"You work here?"

"What can we do? Dreams are one thing, necessities quite another."

It didn't look like failing to become the biggest Catalan Marxist had put a chip on his shoulder. And here I was with another one of those miraculous coincidences, the kind if you tell people about, they don't believe you.

"Let's go have a cup of coffee, kid! We have a lot of things to talk about. I'm back with Rosa again. Why don't you come over for dinner today? Rosa will be ecstatic. We're expecting a baby."

"Are you a big shot around here?" I asked out of self interest.

"I'm *the* big shot!" he answered, mockingly.

"Then before we go for coffee, you'll have to help me solve a problem."

He gave me the best car they had, and didn't even take a deposit. When the guy gave me the keys, red as a beet, I flipped him the bird.

Rosa looked like an elephant, a happy one. It was an extraordinary evening, full of memories and recoveries. They both knew what everyone in the group was doing. I was the only one they'd lost track of. I was always the maverick among the university gang. There were still real class divisions in those days. These days, too, but now there wasn't so much of a difference between someone who ran a car rental agency and a snoop. As a matter of fact, none of them had really made their mark on the world; it seemed they hadn't even had a nibble at the great life they had seemed about to gobble up. So the evening left a bad taste in my mouth. When I went home, I wished I'd never left Majorca, I wished I'd never tried to do the big things in life, biting off more than I could chew. My jaws were tired.

Maybe I wouldn't go to Majorca for just a week. Maybe I'd go back for good.

Troubled and sad, feeling like a failure, I went up the elevator at home, opened the door, went to take a leak, turned on the water in the bathtub, tossing in a handful of bath salts. I went to the kitchen to make tea with honey, got undressed, got my robe and slippers ready, and while the bathtub was filling up, I opened the windows to air out the stuffy house.

When I got into the tub, the sensations of the evening went up in smoke, and I felt mentally nauseated. My throat tightened up, full of tears, and I thought life wasn't worth living and I should do like Sebastiana.

I emptied the tub, drank the tea and hit the sack, wrapped in sadness. Before falling asleep I thought surely I was feeling that way because my period was about to come. Or because I was getting old and I needed company.

Friday morning

I got there just as the employee was opening the door to the inside. Gaudí hadn't come down yet, and when the guy called her on the inside line, she appeared uncombed, wrapped in her satin crepe robe.

"Are you sure that the photo was taken the 15th of May?" she asked as I was giving her Jovel's address.

"Yes. Why?"

"Just a coincidence."

"With what?"

"It doesn't matter," she said distractedly. And after she'd looked with exaggerated attention at the name and address I'd given her, she said, "Did you bring the bill?"

I gave her the bill, ready to really let her have it at the first sign of haggling. But she didn't blink.

"Do you want a check or cash?"

"Do you have that much in cash? There are lots of thieves in Barcelona."

"My employee can go to the bank in no time."

I hesitated a minute. Quim was supposed to go to the bar to start the watch. But if he wasn't there yet, I'd have to leave the post vacant for a few minutes because if she gave me a check, I'd go cash it immediately, just in case. And if the guy went to the bank, I'd have to stay with her for a while, which I didn't like at all; we'd have to talk and at the moment I preferred not to. But the idea of having those hot bills in my hands won me over.

"Okay, cash then."

"She wrote out a check for 400,000 pessetes and called the employee.

"Would you excuse me? I'm going to dress. If anyone comes in, would you mind asking them to wait a few seconds?"

I snooped around the hodge-podge in the store. There really

were extraordinary things. Weird things—I'd like to have known what they were. In one case there was a collection of dressing table items, lipstick among them.

I went straight to the front door. Suddenly I realized that while I was poking around with that junk, she could leave through the apartment door without me seeing her.

The clerk was already coming back. And the door between the landing and the stairs to the store was opening.

He gave Gaudí the envelope, and she gave it to me.

"Count it."

"No need. Listen, how much is this lipstick?"

She opened the case and took it out. She opened it: the owner had used it up down to the bone. I smelled what was left: a rotten smell. But it was gorgeous.

"Fifteen thousand," Gaudí said.

"Holy Christ!"

"It's a unique piece. Do you like it?"

"It's fantastic. But I'm still not crazy enough to spend that kind of money. Even as rich as I am at the moment . . . "

"Take it. Think of it as a tip."

It was the first time in my life anyone had ever given me a tip. It was always the other way around.

XVI

Friday afternoon

I can understand why Quim didn't recognize her. If I hadn't seen her leave from a door that I knew only she could come out of, and if I hadn't been on the alert for any change in appearance, I might have let her get away myself. And I'd seen her face-to-face less than an hour ago.

Everything I'd imagined behind her usual appearance was now on display, put together with artistry and skill. Even Quim's description fell short. I'd have to ask her how she could change so much in such a short time not only out of professional curiosity, but also to learn how myself. She's what men who were somewhat older would call a real classy lady, maybe not the type today's young men would like, but men over fifty would be crazy about her. Pierre Jovel was just in that range.

I wondered which was her usual appearance: this one, or the way she had dressed when she came to my office. If she usually got so gussied up to go out, why hadn't she done that when she came to hire me? Because I was a woman so it wasn't necessary? And why didn't she dress like that in the store, which is where she really needed to look outstanding? Maybe for the antique business a severe look is more appropriate than a totally sophisticated one.

Too many questions for that early in the morning, especially with my head full of fluff from having slept like a log for ten hours.

I waited for a moment in the doorway to the bar to give her a little distance before I started following her. Quim had to rush to the cathedral with the car to have it ready. She wouldn't get away from us this time.

She went towards the taxi stand and I went to the car. I got behind the wheel and we started the chase up Laietana Avenue.

It was going to be a horrendous day.

"If I ever win the lottery, I'm going to get a car with air-conditioning," Quim said.

"And a telephone."

"No matter how much you make fun of me."

Downtown Barcelona was impossible. People went crazy on Fridays. You could see there was a crisis because fewer people were leaving town for their vacations; more were trying to vacation in the city. But still, I was having a good time. Following cars is what I like best about the job. Maybe because it's the sport I'm best at and I feel confident.

The Diagonal was slow, and the taxi driver was driving like an idiot. Why did he have to weave in and out of the lane that was reserved just for him and buses?

Beyond Macià Plaza things thinned out, and after we turned right, the city seemed deserted. And following a car became dangerous.

"The taxi driver is lost, he doesn't know this area. There's a more direct way to get to Jovel's house," I commented. Quim's reply was to blow a big bubble with the gum he was chewing. Big baby.

"Why are you leaving him now?" he asked, surprised when he saw I was turning. The bubble broke, leaving gum all over his face.

Without answering, I went directly to Jovel's address. A few minutes after we parked, the taxi stopped in front of the door. Gaudí got out and the taxi driver waited until she entered.

"Isn't she gorgeous?" Quim commented.

"You're old fashioned. At your age you should like a different type of woman."

"How old do you think I am?"

I really didn't know. I figured he was about five years younger than me. But I'd never asked him.

"Come on, don't be a flirt. Only men pushing fifty ask that question."

The conversation stopped there. I wondered what her secret was to have all doors opened to her so easily. What really linked her to the three men she'd had me find, and whom she'd contacted so quickly afterwards?

Half an hour later, a taxi stopped in front of the door. She came out ten minutes after that, and we were heading for Barcelona again.

The difference in the temperature and density of the air between the higher and lower zones of the city was incredible. Around the cathedral, the mugginess was unbearable. And the tourists in their shorts, noisy and absent-minded, made the heated stones of the entire neighborhood tremble.

Quim and I went back to the bar and the car. But Gaudí didn't go out again all day. I only had one difficulty: the clerk came into the bar, and I had to hide in the bathroom. I didn't want him to see me. At midafternoon, another problem: the people in the bar started joking around with us, making fun of our comings and goings. We'd have to change our observation site.

Nothing until ten at night.

She was wearing a black dress that went from mid-chest to toes, and sandals with heels so high I wouldn't have dared to stand up in them.

The taxi stopped at Castelldefels, in front of a place hidden by pine trees. At the door, without any exterior lights, were two security guards from Rec.

Quim mentioned that he'd heard about a private club out here, where only members could go in. A high rent club.

Around 12:00, the Filipino dressed in white got out of a car. Behind him, three half dressed girls.

"This is the guy Berta told you castrated Antal, right?" Quim asked.

"Berta said he was the procurer of the Filipino girls, and the boyfriend of one of them. I'm the one who thinks it's this guy. But there's something that doesn't tie in."

"What?"

"If he castrated Antal and let him bleed to death, how come

his partners haven't bumped him off?"

"Maybe the partners were interested in Antal's death."

"Exactly."

In the wee hours there was a change of guard. One of the ones who was getting off went to the parking lot, got into a car and drove it to the front door. Jovel and Gaudí got in a second later.

We took off after them. As we went along the coast at Garraf, I realized the same car was continuously behind us. I slowed down at the first passing zone. The car passed me.

"Whew," said Quim.

I liked to walk around the residential neighborhoods of Sitges early in the season. And the beach here was where my room-mates and I had taken our first dip. We didn't like it as much as the beaches on Majorca—that's how Majorcans are—but of all the places on the coast near Barcelona it was the nicest. Then they went back to the island for the summer, and I went swimming here whenever I could. It had been five years now since I'd been back here.

Now, one of the guards went in to the house ahead of them, opened the door and turned on the lights. The other one waited outside. We had parked at the corner of the mansion facing theirs, and when the guard noticed us, Quim and I became a pair of lovers looking for a dark place. But he had no mercy; he threw us out. He said, without waiting for an answer, that we could go be pigs on some other street.

As we were leaving, the other guard came out of the house, and the two got into the car we thought was following us in Gar-raf, parked in front of the house.

I stopped the car in back of the house. The enormous garden was illuminated from the parterres by those ultra tacky green lights. Inside the house, a turn of the century building that didn't deserve such trashy treatment, there were lights in some of the windows. But you really couldn't see inside because nothing but the light itself passed through the curtains.

I waited for a while—don't let me get out until twenty minutes have gone by, I'd told Quim to control my impatience —and then, with the spray in one pocket and the electric poker in the other—I have to admit that these baggy pants with supposedly decorative pockets on the legs served me well on that occasion—I jumped over the hedge of trimmed cypresses. A meowing cat jumped from behind an oleander and hid among some rosebushes. I crouched behind the same oleander and waited. All was silent at the entry gate. A woman's laughter could be heard from inside.

I went along the length of the back wall of the house without finding an open window, or one that would be easy to open. The conversation inside, at a murmur, was coming from a side window. As I was approaching it, a curtain came fluttering out. Jovel was opening the shutter of one of the windows. I kept quiet as a stone.

The uncorking made a jolly sound; a car door opened quickly on the street. The two guards came into the garden and ran, pistol in hand, towards the front door. As they were yanking the door open I took advantage and hid behind a row of fescues, which didn't really hide me, but from there I could see inside the house.

Jovel and Gaudí, with champagne glasses in their hands, looked surprised at the sudden interruption with pistols. Jovel got furious at the two bodyguards, and treated them like imbeciles for being unable to distinguish the sound of a Smith & Wesson from a Moët et Chandon. He spoke a Spanish heavy with rolled r's.

The two watchdogs left with their tails between their legs, muttering damn it, you could have told us you were going to open a bottle of champagne.

Gaudí raised her cup in a toast, laughing, and drank it slowly. With her fixed eyes full of promises. The man left my field of vision and Gaudí put something in her glass and refilled it with champagne. When he returned to the window, she had let her dress fall to the floor and received him with open arms. In the middle of the embrace, she offered him her glass, and he drank the whole thing. He made a face, let go of her, went to the table, grabbed the cork, sniffed it, and threw it down. Then he came back to the antique dealer and, embracing, the two of them disappeared from my field of vision.

I realized that for some time now a cricket had been drilling my ear.

I heard footsteps from the other side of the trimmed cypresses, and voices. It was the two guards, making their rounds around the house. When they got to the back they'd see the car, and Quim, all alone. And they'd come looking for me. Damn their balls!

But they didn't go all the way around. It was too quiet for them to be concerned. When they were in front of the window again they stopped. Between the window and them, with only the thick but fragile separation offered by the cypresses, was me. One of them commented how lucky the rich were, to be able to afford expensive whores. They went on by, mumbling about the lot of the poor.

I heard a car door closing. I waited a few minutes before crossing a bit of garden between the fescues and the window.

As I was doing that, Gaudí appeared, wearing only her birthday suit. She picked her dress up from the floor and her purse from an armchair.

I stretched myself out on the ground, squeezed up against the wall under the windowsill. I heard her approach, breathing just above my head. I heard her going the other way; the living room door opened and closed.

She turned towards the door and looked at me, full of terror mixed with resolve. When she recognized me, all I could see in her eyes was rage.

Jovel was stretched out on the bed with his balls hanging out, sleeping deeply. Or dead? I looked at his chest a second: he was breathing.

Gaudí was dressed, with a scalpel in her hand. Then she grabbed her purse from the night table and took a little pistol out of it.

"If you fire, those guys outside will come in," I said.

"No. They'll think it's another bottle of champagne, and they won't want to risk making themselves ridiculous again."

"I wouldn't want to try it, if I were you."

"Doesn't matter. I'll have time to do my job before they get up here."

"But you won't have time to get away."

How many faces did she have, anyway? Because now she wasn't the one who had come to see me, nor the one I had gone to visit in the store, nor the one who had fooled Quim, nor the one I had seen leaving the apartment today. She was someone else. A woman determined to do what she had to do, as if some inner force wouldn't let her avoid it.

"What is it you're trying to do? Do you want another assassination on your shoulders?"

"I didn't kill the other two. I just castrated them."

She was so elegant in that black silk sheath. And here she was telling me she had castrated two men in the same tone in which she'd told me the price of the lipstick that morning.

"But why?"

"The fifteenth of May, those three men forced me into an entryway and they raped me. One after the other."

Her voice was cold, toneless. It took my breath away. I thought about Sebastiana. But she didn't give me time to think.

"And I decided to castrate them, one after the other. And if you try to stop me, I'll shoot, believe me. I don't want to kill anyone, but if I have to, I will."

"But you let the other two die . . . and made it look like an accident. You didn't want the ones who were left to know they'd been castrated, right?"

"That's not true. I called Antal's wife and told her her husband had had an accident. She had plenty of time to send for help. If she didn't do it . . . I also called Gòmara's house. Castration doesn't make you bleed so fast that there's not time to save you. I'm well informed about that. I even have the emergency telephone number here at Sitges."

I didn't say anything. I wondered how I could distract her. I tried to put my hand into the pocket on my right leg.

"Don't move, Miss Guiu. I'll shoot," she paused again. "Besides, I didn't want the other two to die. I wanted them to remember all their lives that they had raped me. Their deaths keep me from having total revenge. I hope I can accomplish it with this one."

That cricket kept on drilling in my ear. Or was it another one? The serenity of the night out there had become irritating. Or was it my own eardrum that was creaking?

"What about the art smuggling?"

"Sorry, all lies. I had never seen them before. When they left me thrown into the doorway, I still had the strength to follow them. I saw them get into a green metallic car, parked at the plaza San Jaume."

"You can't park at the plaza San Jaume," I said, stupidly.

"At night you can do anything. Even rape."

"Why didn't you go to the police?"

"What good would that have done?"

None, of course. Much less with powerful vultures like those. But I wanted to talk to Jovel. I wanted to know all the implications of that gang. Gaudí was obviously just a grain of sand in the gears.

"I've found out a lot of sordid things about these three. And when I've put them all together, he'll go to prison for sure. The rape will be one more thing against him."

"Sordid things? Nothing is more sordid than rape, as far as I'm concerned, Miss Guiu. I told you once before, I'm not interested in their other business deals."

"I am. And if you don't let me talk to Jovel . . . by the way, why didn't you tell me one of them was a foreigner?"

"They didn't talk much when they were raping me. They just grunted like pigs." She gestured with the hand that was holding the scalpel. "Leave, Miss Guiu. The anesthesia won't last all night. Don't make me shoot."

Sebastiana had slept on sheets stained with vomit. They'd tried to rape me twice at Gòmara's. They'd gang-banged Gaudí.

"You can get out the living room window," I said.

"I know."

"The cypress hedge is lower on the back side of the house," I said and walked towards the door. But I turned around. "If you didn't know them before, how did you manage to contact them so easily?"

"I offered works of art to Antal. You'd told me his wife was

150

very fond of them. It wasn't hard to make an appointment with him. I called Gòmara at the number you gave me. I told him who I was, and reminded him of the fifteenth of May. He accepted the date immediately."

"Did you know that Gòmara's body was crushed from waist to knees?"

"The newspapers said he'd died of a heart attack. We met at a hotel in Barcelona. I told him I didn't mind the rape, that I'd even liked it and I wanted to try it again. It was quite easy."

"How about Jovel?"

"In your report you told me he was a museum curator. I told him that they'd offered to sell me a stolen piece, that maybe was from his museum. Antique dealers have all the latest information about those kinds of objets d'art. The museum of Lyon was robbed two years ago. I described the piece to him . . . "

She wasn't lying to me now. And the lies she'd told me up to now were well justified.

"Give me the emergency telephone number," I said.

"What do you want it for?"

"To let them know. That way you can escape faster."

She smiled and gestured towards the purse on the night table.

"Don't try to fool me, Lònia. You can count on me shooting."

I rummaged through the bag.

"I'm not giving you much time. I'll look for a booth, and I'll call them within ten minutes."

I closed the door softly.

When I went back towards the house after I called, all the lights were still on and the two cars were in the same place, right in front of the garden gate.

When the ambulance siren silenced all the crickets in the world, the two watchdogs jumped out of their car.

I looked at my watch. Elena Gaudí still had plenty of time to get a taxi at the stand in front of the church.

When the ambulance people and the guards entered the house, I slipped silently two blocks away to where Quim was waiting for me with the car.

"You drive, Quim. I'm tired."

EPILOGUE

Sunday

We met at the same restaurant where we'd met three years ago. He had a few grays around the temples; he was thinner.

"I'm on a diet. Triglicerides."

"What's that?" I laughed.

"Ailments of age. Don't pay any attention," he said.

"I think you look great..."

It was true. He didn't knock you over, but when you looked at him for a while, you saw he was good-looking. My mom would have said he was dashing and affable.

He waited for me to speak. Maybe he was a little shy.

"I saw you at Antal's funeral. Felip Antal."

I'd caught him with his pants down. He didn't have time to hide his surprise. But he took the bull by the horns immediately.

"What were you doing there? Are you a friend of the Baroness?"

"No, not me. What about you?"

"I was a friend of Felip."

"No kidding!"

"Yes, it's true. We were in the army together."

"But he was older than you are!"

"He'd kept getting deferments. I tried too, but I didn't get them."

"One of those friendships that lasts, huh?"

"Not really," he shrugged his shoulders. "We kept in contact because we both liked music. He organized chamber music concerts at his house."

"I see. He died from a violin attack."

"You invited me to dinner to talk about Felip Antal?"

"Yes."

He looked at me mockingly, and I was about to send him packing. I had the feeling I was sticking my neck out, but I had come to a decision: Arquer was the best snoop in Barcelona and one of the best for miles around. He liked the business, much more than I did; he really had a vocation for it.

Maybe he knew as much as I did, or more, and then I'd make an ass of myself. But if he didn't, he'd surely be interested in the case. And we could make a deal that would be mutually advantageous.

"Antal didn't die by accident."

"He didn't?"

"You know it as well as I do. Or do you think I swallowed that stuff about the military and the concerts?"

"It's up to you."

What a scoundrel.

"But maybe you didn't know that Gòmara, Ernest Gòmara, the guy with the wood business, didn't die of a heart attack either."

I could see from the effort he was making to hide it that he didn't know what I was talking about. I attacked the beet steak with a sense of satisfaction.

"I think it's ridiculous for you vegetarians to call your dishes carnivorous names. That's a beet pie."

"Don't change the subject, Lluís. Or don't you want to know what your friend Antal died of?"

"I know what he died of," he said seriously.

"What?"

"They castrated him."

"Christ!"

He knew. But what he knew was Berta Prat's version. Or at least that's what he told me. The Baroness had told him that her husband had died accidentally. He suspected that maybe it wasn't so accidental, and he'd done his own investigation, at his own risk, at the Garbí Clinic. And when the Baroness found out, she told him the truth.

"Did she tell you anything about the Orient Sunshine Company?"

He shook his head yes. But it was obvious he didn't want to talk about things he didn't know about.

"Have you been reading the papers?"

"What are you getting at, Lónia? You're spoiling my supper."

"Have you read about the death of the French mafioso Pierre Jovel?"

"A settling of accounts, you can see from a mile away," he finished his last bite of beet pie. "Leukemia, indeed!"

"He was castrated, too. And Gòmara."

He looked at me in silence, like a nun who wants to look very strict and doesn't quite know how, as if he wanted to bawl me out for my frivolity.

"Lònia, what are you trying to tell me? What do you know?"

"What do you know?"

"No more than I just told you."

It was tough for a pro like him to admit he knew so little.

Parsimoniously, I started to dish out the second course. Then I handed him the oil and vinegar set. He stared at me, and his eyebrows seemed to have suddenly gotten thicker. I started to eat.

"Are you going to tell me something, or not?"

"Yes, but I want something in return."

"What?"

"I know some things about the market in Filipino girls. But that's nothing compared to some other smuggling. I know some things about Jovel. Maybe not everything, but enough to cause some trouble."

"He's dead."

"I know. And I know who killed him."

"The international mafia," he said with his mouth full of grated carrot.

"Exactly. And our very own mafia. Interested?"

"Why do you want to tell me? If you have proof, it would mean a great professional coup."

"I know. But there's a personal matter involved, or two. And I'm sick of it. I want to go to an island."

"Too much for you, huh?" his voice took on a paternal tone. I didn't answer. He kept on eating carrots. "And you want to pass the case on to me so I can clarify things, right?"

"Everything's clear. And I don't want to pass it on to you. I want to sell it to you."

"Sell it?"

"Yes, generosity is one of my virtues."

"Okay, tell me the price first."

"An airplane ticket."

"To Majorca?"

"A little bit further. With discretion as a tip."

"You don't want to be involved."

"Me and another woman—both in need of discretion."

"The one who killed Jovel?"

"The one who castrated Antal, Gòmara, and Jovel."

He had to close his mouth so he wouldn't lose the mouthful. But the fork made a lot of noise as it hit the ground. When the waiter had brought him another one, Lluís Arquer was still staring at me, perplexed.

"Haven't you ever noticed the graffiti done in lilac saying 'Against rape, castration'?"

"Yes, and I think it's barbarous."

"Me too." I thought of Sebastiana and I wasn't so sure of my affirmation, but I didn't dare argue. I said, "Well, this woman made those words a reality."

"And that person is Lònia Guiu. That's why you want to get away from here."

I froze. That asshole could turn me in. I regretted having called him. But I'd already brought him aboard. I jolted.

"No, not me. But you can think whatever you want, I won't tell you who she is. Because if they'd done to me what they did to her I would have done exactly the same thing. And I want to leave so I won't be tempted to do it."

"But did you get raped or not?" he was exasperated.

"No. But a fifteen year old girl got raped, and she killed herself... at my house."

"What were the three of them doing at your house?"

I burst out laughing. I'd bewildered him.

"No, those three weren't at my house, and they raped a forty year old woman, not a fifteen year old girl. And the woman didn't kill herself, she castrated them. They're two different cases that got mixed up in my life. That's why I'm fed up."

"Why do you want to pass them on to me? They're closed cases."

"No, Lluís dear. There's a juicy pot of stew left behind Antal, Gòmara and Jovel. That's what I want to sell you. In exchange for a trip and for you forgetting about the rapes and deballings. They aren't any good to you, though they led me to unraveling the whole thing."

We finished dining and looked for a cool, quiet place. A discreet, dark bar, ideal for confidentialities. He treated me to a bottle of French champagne. When I tasted it—for the first time in my life—I understood why the Detective Association's champagne had tasted like horse piss.

"A woman hired me to look for three men. All she gave me was a license number and a rotten lie as her motive. The car belonged to Antal. I discovered, following a hunch I'd gotten when I was looking around at Antal's company . . . "

"You go on hunches?" he said mockingly.

"Don't interrupt me. In any case, I found out that Antal had something to do with the procurement of Filipino prostitutes. I gave Antal's address to my client, and before the week was out he had died accidentally. I suspected my client, but I kept on looking for the two other men. I found Gòmara at Antal's funeral. And at his factory, they gave me a royal greeting. They put me under, stole my documents and half destroyed my car—a couple of heavies dressed in uniforms from a security guard company belonging to Antal. At Gòmara's factory I discovered a shipment that had just arrived from the Philippines. Officially it was wood. But eucalyptus weighs a lot less than the wood they had declared on the shipping invoices. So there had to be something heavy underneath the wood: for example, guns from the U.S. Army with photocopies of sheets of instructions on how to assemble them. My visit to the Gòmara factory won me the visit of two cops—I have their identification numbers—and I had to move my office. But I'll spare you the trivia." I took a long sip of champagne to clear my voice and I continued, "At Gòmara's, I found more papers, more invoices of other shiploads, imports and exports, names of ships. I consulted with a friend of mine who works with that sort of thing, and I snooped around the international docks. In a shipload sent by Gòmara Wood to the

Philippines, there were some little bottles with a mysterious liquid, which turned out to be an extremely powerful poison... which, curiously, is made at the Garbí Clinic."

"You mean... "

"Yes, dear. Chemical weapons. Well, one of the elements. In the clinic storeroom, guarded by security guards from Rec, they keep the materials, and they do the preparation in the laboratory. Treated conveniently at the point of arrival, it becomes an invention that makes you ashamed of belonging to the human race. And it's easy to get the material—well, relatively, since they use so much they probably need special permission..."

Lluís was gulping down champagne nonstop. He ordered another bottle.

"I gave Gòmara's address to my client, and what do you know, he bites the dust too... and at the Garbí Clinic. The morgue was closed but I broke in. The cadaver was smashed from the waist to the knees. Something very heavy had gone over his middle and flattened him. But his file and the death certificate said heart attack. That's when I found out that Antal had also ended up at that clinic, after his 'accident.' And then I spoke with Dr. Canal, and I found an invoice in his office like the ones at Gòmara's. That's when they explained to me the same version of Antal's death that the Baroness told you."

"Why didn't you watch your client?"

"I did. But I left a man in charge of it, and he fucked up."

Lluís laughed wryly.

"But the third man was missing. I found him with photographs. He was at an international symposium. Among those attending were Antal, Gòmara, Dr. Canal, the supposed castrator of Antal, who claims, of course to be in charge of Rec Security, but in fact he gets girls, Filipinos like himself, for the Castelldefels Cerós Club... and as guardians, two security guards from Rec. Well, from the photos, my client recognized the third man, and I looked into who he was. A real big shot in the art collectors' world. And this time I did follow my client myself. I found her with scalpel in hand, about to castrate Jovel. All her lies and inconsistencies were cleared up now. She didn't know the three men at all. They'd just come out of the feast that ended the symposium, and they grabbed her and forced her into a doorway and raped her, one after the other. And the woman castrated them, one after the other."

"Wait a minute, wait a minute! There's something that doesn't fit in, Lònia."

"Everything fits in. Everything. Think about it a minute and you'll see. And if we come to an agreement, I'll write it all down for you, with all the details, and you'll see there aren't any loose ends."

"What doesn't fit is that those three men . . . they were gangsters, all right, but not ne'er-do-wells."

"So?"

"I mean I can't believe three fat cats like those would spend their time raping forty year-old women in dark doorways of Barcelona. What's the need?"

I burst out laughing. He'd said just what I expected, exactly when I expected it. And it was more or less the same comment Quim had made. Reasoning that had made its mark on me, to the point where I began to wonder if the antique dealer had fooled me again.

But I'd spoken with Mercè about it, and I went to dinner with Arquer well prepared. While I put a pile of photocopies in front of Lluís, I repeated Mercè's words:

"That's a typical male argument, Lluís. Men think other men are rapists only if they're ne'er-do-wells in general, or mentally ill. Look at those reports . . . "

Lluís Arquer looked through the photocopies Mercè had given me. They were cases collected by the WPS, a non-governmental organization with international branches, affiliated with UNESCO and WHO. Lluís' face changed as he leafed through the papers. At one point, as if to cover up how disturbed he was, he asked,

"What is this WPS?"

"Women's Protection Society."

"Are all these cases true?"

"True and proven. And all from last year."

"Balls! Men really are beasts."

"Not all, fortunately," I conceded, generously.

They were cases of specific men, all well off, without problems, who had raped at some point; all over the world, with no distinction of age or race.

Lluís was overwhelmed.

"What animals, my god!"

"And that's not counting husbands who rape their wives every day . . . "

"Come on Lònia, no feminist sermons. I have enough with these papers."

"So, everything ties in, now?"

He didn't answer. He returned the photocopies in silence, drank another glass of champagne, and looked at me.

"Okay, what else?"

"Where were we in the story?"

"The woman was castrating them, one after the other . . . "

"Right. And after she'd castrated them, she called their homes immediately, because she didn't want them to die. She didn't want her vengeance to end with that violent act. She wanted them to remember all their lives . . . "

"Which means women can be beasts too."

"I can't deny that."

"Okay, she didn't want them to die, but the fact is they died, right?"

"The fact is they died. Antal done in, Gòmara smashed . . . "

"What about Jovel? Did you keep him from getting castrated?"

"No. I let her accomplish her task of vengeance. I called the ambulance myself. Except that Jovel, naturally, ended up at the Garbí Clinic, where he died of leukemia. Or whatever, I haven't dug into that. The fact is, he died. And I can assure you there was plenty of time to stop the hemorrhaging. My client assured me of that, and I later confirmed it myself. That means Dr. Canal knows perfectly well what the three of them died of, and why."

"That's a fib, Lónia."

"You know perfectly well it isn't. I have all the papers to prove it. Shipments from the Philippines to Barcelona. Shipments from Barcelona to the Philippines and Africa. Three dead men, who could have been eunuchs. Oh, by the way, I had to leave the Garbí Clinic running like mad, pursued by the same two cops who made the threatening visit to my office. The same cops that arrested my partner, accusing him of armed robbery at Gòmara's. And Dr. Canal... "

"Is getting married to the Baroness of Prenafeta."

"I know."

We drank our last glass.

"Are you sure you want to turn this over to me? No matter how expensive the plane tickets are, it's still a gift to me."

"You're so nice. Cheers."

Lluís asked the waiter for the bill and a telephone.

"Pepa? Yes, I know, I know. Okay, okay, are you listening to me now? Good, good kid. Before you come to the office tomorrow, go to a travel agency and buy a ticket to Australia... Yes, yes, kangaroos... No, not in my name... What do I care what company?... No, listen, in the name of Apol.lònia Guiu... Yes, Apol.lònia, with the l split. Good night, honey."

"It didn't have to be for tomorrow. I still have to prepare all the papers."

As we said goodnight, out on the street, I said to him,

"If you find my car at Gòmara's, get it back for me and give it to my partner. I'll bring you all the papers tomorrow."

Closed for Vacation. The door to the stairway was locked, too. I opened it with my own skeleton key.

There was a paper hanging on her wall, written with a heavy black labeler: May fifteenth.

I found what I was looking for in the secretary in the little waiting room: all the reports, notes and pictures I'd given her. The desk calendar, stopped in May, had the 15th circled in red.

I took the opportunity to snoop around a little. The bathroom mirror was marked with lipstick: May 15th.

I sat for a moment on the King's sofa. On the little table in the center there was a package with my name on it. How did she know I'd come to her place?

I opened the package. It was a little wooden modernist statue. There was an envelope in its hands, with a card inside which said: Thank you. Signed Elena Gaudí. Dated the 15th of May.

I went to the office to get Arquer's dossier ready. All the other documentation on the case went into the bathroom sink, which the fire cracked. The same thing had happened to the sink in the Majorcan apartment when they came to arrest Margalida and the others didn't want any compromising papers to be found on them.

I wrote a letter to Quim, and one to Mercè.

Day was breaking when I left the office. I still had time. I went down to the breakwater. The sea was calm, silvery. I missed Majorca again. But it passed quickly. After all, Australia was an island too.

About the Translator

Kathleen McNerney is a professor of Spanish and Catalan at the West Virginia University. She edited the non-Castilian materials in *Women Writers of Spain* (Greenwood Press, 1986), and an anthology of Catalan women's fiction entitled *On Our Own Behalf* to be published in 1988 by the University of Nebraska Press.

About the Author

Maria-Antònia Oliver was born in Manacor, Majorca, Spain in 1946. She has published six novels as well as translating, among other works, *The Years* by Virginia Woolf, *Moby Dick* and *Tom Sawyer* into Catalan. She currently divides her time between Majorca and Barcelona.

Selected Titles From Seal Press
Mysteries/International Women's Crime Series

ANTIPODES by Maria-Antònia Oliver (Spain) $8.95,
0-931188-82-2. Lonia stumbles onto an international prostitution
ring and plunges headfirst into an intrigue of dramatic proportions.

HALLOWED MURDER by Ellen Hart. $8.95, 0-931188-83-0.
Sororities can be deadly: Jane Lawless goes after the murderer.

THE DOG COLLAR MURDERS by Barbara Wilson. $8.95,
0-931188-69-5. Pam Nilsen solves the murder of an anti-pornography
activist. Third in the series.

SISTERS OF THE ROAD by Barbara Wilson. $8.95, 0-931188-45-8.
Pam Nilsen looks for a teenage prostitute. Second in series.

MURDER IN THE COLLECTIVE by Barbara Wilson. $8.95,
0-931188-23-7. A lesbian and a leftist collective merge—to murder.
First in the Pam Nilsen series.

LADIES' NIGHT by Elisabeth Bowers. $8.95, 0-931188-65-2.
P.I. Meg Lacey tackles a child-pornography ring in Vancouver.

FIELDWORK by Maureen Moore. $8.95, 0-931188-54-7. Single
mother Marsha Lewis investigates murder as part of her college
degree.

GLORY DAYS by Rosie Scott (New Zealand). $8.95,
0-931188-72-5. A glorious heroine in a drug and kidnapping mystery.

THE LAST DRAW by Elizabeth Peterzen (Sweden). $8.95,
0-931188-67-9. A psychological puzzle that will leave you stunned.

SEAL PRESS, founded in 1976 to provide a forum for women writers
and feminist issues, has many other titles in stock: fiction, self-help
books, anthologies and translations. Any of the books above may be
ordered from us at 3131 Western Ave, Suite 410, Seattle WA 98121
(include $2.00 for the first book and .50 for each additional book).
Write to us for a free catalog or if you would like to be on our mailing
list.